Backpacking in Chile

Steve Hänisch

Backpacking in Chile by Steve Hänisch

Steve Hänisch
Barmbeker Straße 85
22303 Hamburg
Email: steve@back-packer.org
Website: www.back-packer.org

All rights reserved.

No part of this book may be reproduced in any form or by any electronic or mechanical means including information storage and retrieval systems without permission in writing from the author. The only exception is by a reviewer, who may quote short excerpts in a review.

All Photos by Steve Hänisch

Although the author and publisher have made every effort to ensure that the information in this book was correct at press time, the author and publisher do not assume and hereby disclaim any liability to any party for any loss, damage, or disruption caused by errors or omissions, whether such errors or omissions result from negligence, accident, or any other cause.

The information provided within this book is for general informational purposes only. While we try to keep the information up-to-date and correct, there are no representations or warranties, express or implied, about the completeness, accuracy, reliability, suitability or availability with respect to the information, products, services, or related graphics contained in this book for any purpose. Any use of this information is at your own risk.

The authors and publisher advise readers to take full responsibility for their safety and know their limits. Before practicing the outdoor activities described in this book, be sure that your equipment is well maintained, and do not take risks beyond your level of experience, aptitude, training, and comfort level.

ISBN: 1545126313
ISBN-13: 978-1545126318

Second edition, April 2017
Copyright © 2017 by Steve Hänisch

TABLE OF CONTENTS

    Preface

1 Preparation   **1**

    What to Expect in Chile   2

    The Weather in Chile   2

    Top 5 in Chile   3

    Language & Communication   4

    Safety   4

    Chilean cuisine   5

    Budget & Prices   6

    Health & Insurance   7

    Entry Requirements & Custom Regulations   7

    Transportation   8

    Accommodation   10

    My South America Packing List   11

2 Map & Itineraries   **17**

    (A) Volcanoes, Coast & Desert in 2 or 3 Weeks   19

    (B) Carretera Austral in 2 or 3 Weeks   25

    (C) Carretera Austral & Patagonia in 5 Weeks   33

    (D) Best of Patagonia in 3 Weeks (very active)   37

3 Travel Guides   **41**

    San Pedro de Atacama   43

Santiago	49
Valparaiso & Vina del Mar	53
Pucón	57
Puerto Varas & Puerto Montt	61
The Carretera Austral (Overview)	67
Chaitén	71
Puyuhuapi	77
Coyhaique & Cerro Castillo	81
Puerto Rio Tranquilo	87
Cochrane & Tortel	93
Villa O'Higgins	97
Puerto Natales	103
Punta Arenas	107
My personal Chile Insider Tips	111
4 Trekking Guide Carretera Austral	**113**
1) Day hike to Cerro Castillo	114
2) Day Hike to Mirador Altavista	115
3) Border Crossing Villa O'Higgins - El Chaltén	116
5 Trekking Guide Torres del Paine	**123**
Preparation	124
Patagonia Packing List for Trekking & Camping	135
Trekking Guide "W" Route	141

	Trekking Guide "O" / Circuit Route	149
6	**Additional Resources**	**161**
	All URLs mentioned in this book	161
	Recommended Guidebooks	161
	Recommended Maps	163
	Other Guide Books from Me	164
7	**About the Author**	**165**

Steve Hänisch

PREFACE

First of all, thanks for buying this book!

My name is Steve and I've been living in and traveling through Chile for several months on my trips in 2010, 2013, and recently in 2016. On my journeys, I visited the tourist hot spots and many lesser-known places in the country. Especially during my two hitchhiking adventures along the Carretera Austral, I went to places that are totally off the beaten path.

I summed up all my experiences, recommendations, itineraries, and even detailed route descriptions of the most stunning hikes in this handy book. Though I can't offer the range of a „Lonely Planet", you'll find truly honest and very personal recommendations in this guidebook that will answer most of your questions and guide you to places not many travelers have been to.

My mission is to help you to make the best out of your time in this beautiful country. Enjoy your time and help me spread the word by recommending this guide to fellow travelers and friends. In addition, it would be great if you could leave a review on Amazon!

I highly appreciate your feedback and corrections as prices can change every now and then, especially in South America (please get in touch via email at steve@back-packer.org).

To travel lighter, I also offer the eBook version of this book on request. Unlike the printed book, the eBook has all the links needed and makes it easier to book the recommended accommodations directly. If you want the free eBook, you only need to send me an email with your proof of purchase attached (e.g. screenshot of the invoice from Amazon). I'll get back to you as soon as possible.

Feel free to join my mailing list to receive some additional information and tips for your upcoming trip. You can find the form over at the following website where you can also find all resources for Chile I linked in the book:

www.back-packer.org/chile-book-links/

Safe travels,
Steve

1 PREPARATION

Before starting your adventure, you should get to know some things about the country to which you are about to travel.

I already did most of the research for you — I used the FAQ from the readers of my blog to summarize the most important facts and personal tips regarding the right preparation for a trip to Chile.

Steve Hänisch

What to Expect in Chile

When looking at Chile on a map of South America, you'll quickly realize the diversity awaiting you here: be it in matters of the climate or in matters of the landscape.

With its long and narrow shape, this country is one of the most diverse on the continent—ranging from the driest desert in the world in the north to the glaciers of Patagonia in the very south.

For me, Chile was the first country I traveled to in South America and it is surely one of the best countries to start with coming from Europe or North America.

Chile is often described as the most European country of South America and has the strongest economy, resulting in a good infrastructure and relatively high safety for travelers compared to other South-American countries.

The Chileans are very friendly and welcoming to foreigners, especially if you make the effort to speak/try to speak Spanish. As they are big patriots, they will often ask you about your opinion regarding Chile as a foreigner— you should use this conversation starter and highlight your positive experiences as well as your enthusiasm about traveling through Chile!

The Weather in Chile

Although the weather is as diverse as the country itself, it is safe to say that you'll find the best conditions from October till April. If you plan to stay longer, this should be the timeframe you choose.

Patagonia is a bit rougher than the rest: strong winds, colder temperatures, and quick weather changes are normal down here. This is why the best timeframe to pick for this region is a bit shorter: from December till February/March.

The Atacama Desert can be visited all year round as rain is pretty rare there.

Top 5 in Chile

When looking at the numerous beautiful spots Chile has to offer, it is quite a challenge to pick only five. However, it might help you to make the most out of your time as more often one is not able to visit all places in one trip.

The following five spots are my personal favorites you shouldn't miss when in Chile:

1) Torres del Paine – this National Park in the south is a landmark in Chile. Photos from Torres del Paine are often used as cover photos for travel guides (like this one here. Ha!). The landscape is truly magical and offers much variety in a relatively small area.

2) Atacama desert – in the very north, you'll find a completely different world: stone deserts, salt flats, lagoons, geysers, volcanoes, and flamingos.

3) Pucón – located in northern part of the south, it is a perfect fit for outdoor lovers. The highlight: climbing the active volcano, Villarrica.

4) Valparaiso – this port city close to Santiago is part of the UNESCO World Cultural Heritage: Street-art, colorful houses located on the many hills connected by rack railways make this spot a picturesque one to visit.

5) Carretera Austral – This attraction is a true challenge as it is hard to access. Nevertheless, it is rewarding if you take the time and effort to do so. I hitchhiked the whole Route 7 within three weeks and saw marble caves, rainforests, fjords, and glaciers in the most remote areas of Patagonia. This adventure is totally worth it!

Language & Communication

Before embarking on my first trip to Chile, I only knew a few words in Spanish but realized quickly that knowing the local lingo was a massive advantage in many situations when traveling.

Despite that English is spoken in tourist centers, such as airports or at tour agencies, you easily run into communication problems on the street or even at bus terminals.

I highly recommend learning at least some basic Spanish—I did so with an online course without previous knowledge and got along quite well with the locals (I used and recommend the service from Babbel, see link list).

As mentioned above, the people are very friendly and patient even if your Spanish isn't perfect. Moreover, Chileans are proud people and will ask you a lot about your opinion of their country — don't offend them.

Safety

If you compare Chile with other South-American countries, it is considered safer than most of the others. Nevertheless, you should be careful in big cities and at night.

Try not to be an easy target by showcasing your belongings in the streets (having your DSLR hanging around your neck/ walking around with the iPad in your hands). Only use it when you need it and make sure to ask in your hostel/hotel which areas to avoid.

In Chile, the bus terminals are hot spots for thieves. This is why you should always watch your bags all al times and never leave them unattended.

Please follow my other instructions given in the article „30 Tips and Ways to Stay Safe While Traveling" which you can find in the link list for this book.

Please also check the official foreign travel advice of your country of residence in matters of safety.

Chilean cuisine

Backpacking in Chile also means you'll eat a lot of meat as the Chileans love to eat 'carne', as well as fast food. One of the most important ingredients in the Chilean cuisine is the avocado ('palta'), which tastes much more intense and is much softer than I was used to.

The most popular dishes are asado (BBQ), Empanadas (stuffed pastries), completos (hot dogs with a big range of toppings), cazuela (soup), and fish (along the coast and in Santiago).

I really liked the meat from the asados. Nevertheless, I was in need of some variation after a few days. If you prefer vegetarian or even vegan dishes, your best bet is the big touristic centers. In Valparaiso and Santiago, you are likely to find suitable restaurants. Apart from that, I recommend grocery shopping and cooking your own meals with fresh vegetables from the farmers' markets or supermarkets to eat more healthily.

For drinks, you should try the national drink Pisco Sour. In addition, the Chilean red wine is a great choice. If you like beer, you'll also find some good brands here—especially the ones from the South ('Austral', 'Kunstmann').

Budget & Prices

Economically, Chile is the most powerful country in South America. The prices are only a little bit below the European standard.

In Patagonia and the Atacama Desert, prices are usually high.

Price ranges:

- Night in a dorm: 11-16 USD
- Night in a private room: 18-27 USD
- Meal in a restaurant: 6-11 USD
- Long-haul bus ticket: 55-65 USD (Santiago-San Pedro, 23h)

I withdrew money from ATM machines with my German DKB credit card (Visa Card), which always worked out very well.

I also advise you to use your credit card for withdrawing cash. Generally, it's not recommended to exchange money as the costs are higher for you.

In this book, I decided to list all prices in US dollars to make it easier for you to budget your trip (apart from Torres del Paine as prices there change every season); the local currency in Chile is the Chilean Peso (CLP).

Health & Insurance

Six months before you leave, you should consult your doctor to check your vaccinations as some regions in South America require special vaccinations before you are granted entry. The earlier you take care of this the better, as some vaccinations need a few months before you gain full protection.

For Chile, you should review and update vaccinations for tetanus, diphtheria, pertussis, measles, mumps, rubella, and polio. If you travel to and from Peru, as well as the Easter Islands, you should also get yellow fever protection.

Please make sure to check the Chile country information over at www.iamat.org for the latest updates and risks.

The hygiene conditions in Chile are mostly not as good as that of other countries, for example, in Western Europe. Be aware and try to avoid drinking tap water.

I highly recommend getting good travel insurance as in almost every case, your current health insurance won't work in Chile.

During my time I used the renowned travel insurance by WorldNomads, which you can easily purchase online for the exact time needed and you'll also have the possibility extend it while traveling (url in link list).

Entry Requirements & Custom Regulations

In most cases, you only need a valid passport to enter Chile as a tourist for a stay of up to 90 days. When entering the country, you need to complete a form and you'll be issued with a 'Tarjeta de Turismo - Tourist Card' that you need to retain and present to the immigration officials when you leave.

If you intend to stay longer, or if you want to study or work in Chile, you usually have to apply for a special Visa. Another option for tourists who plan to extend their stay in Chile would be to leave the country and reenter to get a new tourist Visa (so-called "visa run").

Besides the usual customs regulations, be aware that you're not allowed to bring any fruit, seeds, unprocessed vegetables, or animal products into the country (eat that apple or sandwich before crossing the border).

Find the entry requirements for your nationality on the official sites of your country:

- UK citizens: gov.uk/foreign-travel-advice/chile

- US citizens: travel.state.gov/content/passports/english/country/chile.html

- Canadian citizens: travel.gc.ca/destinations/chile

Transportation

The most budget friendly way to get around is the long-distance buses. Buses in Chile are comfortable and much better than those in Europe. Long trips are comparably cheap and enjoyable (65 USD for a 22h drive).

Bus tickets can be purchased at the bus terminals. Though you sometimes have the option of booking them online, you can get better deals at the counter of the company inside the terminals.

When traveling by bus, you can book different categories (semi-cama = half a bed, cama = bed, Premium). Moreover, snacks, drinks, and movies are included.

The biggest and most popular bus companies are TurBus

(highly recommended!) and Pullmann:

- Tur-Bus Chile: [www.turbus.cl]
  (in Spanish)

- Pullman Bus: [www.ventapasajes.cl/pullmanbus]
  (in Spanish)

Unfortunately, it is pretty difficult to buy bus tickets online as a foreigner without a Chilean ID directly with the bus companies. Luckily, there is a good service that not only makes it possible to buy tickets online but also comes with a user-friendly, English version:

- Recorrido.cl: [www.recorrido.cl/en]

Recently, domestic flights have become more affordable with the budget airline "Sky". As a result of that, new low-cost competitor prices went down and made it worth considering for long distances, e.g. from Santiago to Patagonia or to Calama. This is why often also the big player, Lan Chile, offers good deals.

Here is a small Spanish-English cheat sheet for researching connections online:

- Ciudad de Origen = Origin

- Ciudad de Destino = Destination

- Fecha de Ida = Day of Travel

- Fecha de Regreso = Day of Return

- Horario = Time

- Ida = One Way Trip

- Ida y Vuelta = Return Trip

Accommodation

In Chile, there are several good overnight options. I'll highlight my personal recommendations of places to stay within the travel guide section of this Book including information on prices and services (those are mostly Hostels and Hospedajes).

You can find links for all my recommended Hostels in the link list, sorted by location.

Hostal - the hostels are great and offer many services beyond the usual. Most hostels have private rooms, Wi-Fi is free, and the atmosphere is lovely. A great place to connect with fellow travelers!

Hotels - there is a big network of good hotels of international standard all over Chile.

Hospedaje - these are mostly private rooms available for rent, especially in smaller towns and villages. They are budget friendly and mostly include breakfast.

Hosteria - these are private rooms in restaurants, comparable to the Hospedajes.

Cabaña - In touristic hot spots you are able to rent huts/cabins which can accommodate more people. This is a very popular option amongst Chileans on vacation.

My South America Packing List

The following South America packing list is based on my experience of traveling seven months through South America —from the very hot areas like the Atacama desert down to the windy, but beautiful Patagonia with its amazing glacier landscapes. Therefore, this list is universal and usable for diverse trips, no matter if they are long or short.

You need much less than you might think. Trust me.

During my trip, my luggage became less and less. I got rid of things I never used and focused on essential, lightweight things instead. This list is what I came up with after this process. Don't worry: even if there is something missing for you, you can always buy stuff when you need it. This way you save space and weight.

An online version of this packing list with links to certain products I used can be find in the link list.

1) Backpack & Bags

- [ ] Travel Backpack – the Deuter Aircontact (55-85l) or the Osprey Farpoint 40 (40l) are great choices
- [ ] Daypack – to use for day trips or small hiking tours
- [ ] Drybag – keeps your technical equipment dry
- [ ] ZipLocs bags help you to organise
- [ ] Plastic bags – for shoes and dirty clothes
- [ ] Optional: compression bag to save even more space

2) Clothes

In general, I packed for more or less one week to keep it easy and to leave enough space for other essentials. At the end of the week, I did laundry in the hotel/hostel in which I was staying or went to a laundry center in the city.

Everything related to the outdoors can be found separately within the trekking guide section of this book.

- [ ] 7 x underwear
- [ ] 3 x socks
- [ ] 1 x hiking socks
- [ ] 4 x regular t-shirts
- [ ] 1 x long sleeve
- [ ] 2 x sports t-shirts (mid layer) – I recommend using breathable sports shirts
- [ ] 1 x shirt for dinner & special occasions
- [ ] 1 x shorts
- [ ] 1 x hiking pants, with the option to turn into a short pant
- [ ] 1 x jeans pants
- [ ] 1 x board Shorts, usable for swimming as well as regular shorts
- [ ] 1 x fleece jacket (mid layer) – highly recommended for colder parts and the evenings!
- [ ] 1 x breathable, waterproof jacket as shell layer
- [ ] 1 x pair of flip-flop (e.g. Havaianas)
- [ ] 1 x sneakers – comfy boots for traveling (e.g. Nike Free Run)

3) Toiletries

In this list, I just stick to the basics. You should extend it to your own liking (especially female readers).

- [ ] Hanging toiletry kit
- [ ] 1x toothbrush and toothpaste
- [ ] Deodorant
- [ ] 1x basic skin cream
- [ ] Shower gel
- [ ] Mini fingernail clipper
- [ ] Set of cotton buds
- [ ] 1x sunscreen
- [ ] 1x microfibre towel—dries super fast and is lightweight and small
- [ ] Medicine: headache pills, Imodium, charcoal tablet, and your medicine
- [ ] Travel first-aid kit
- [ ] Optional: comb/hairbrush, hair gel

4) Camera & Technical Gadgets

- [ ] Universal Compact interchangeable lens camera e.g. Sony Alpha Cameras
- [ ] GoPro – great waterproof camera for the outdoors
- [ ] Smartphone or iPod Touch for Apps
- [ ] eReader for eBooks (travel guides) e.g. Kindle eReader

- [ ] Memory cards (take a few with you, especially when you travel without a notebook or HDD)
- [ ] Charger
- [ ] Spare batteries
- [ ] Headphones
- [ ] Waterproof cellphone case
- [ ] External battery – to charge camera/devices
- [ ] Optional: MacBook Air, Lacie external portable HDD

5) Travel Gadgets

- [ ] World Travel Adapter
- [ ] Sleeping mask
- [ ] Earplugs (for use in hostels, planes or buses)
- [ ] Electric outlet wall adapter – mostly there aren't enough plugs when you travel to charge your stuff!
- [ ] Sunglasses – e.g. quality glasses from Ray Ban
- [ ] Padlock – to use for Lockers in Hostels
- [ ] Travel pillow
- [ ] Multi Tool – to fix stuff or for preparing your meal

Backpacking in Chile

6) Documents, Money & Security

Store your important documents safely to avoid getting pickpocketed.

- [ ] Waterproof document bag
- [ ] Passport / visa
- [ ] Plane / bus / train tickets
- [ ] Cash in local currency (mostly you can exchange money at your home airport or bank)
- [ ] Money belt, I'm using the one from Eagle Creek
- [ ] Print of booking confirmation (Tour, Hotel, Transfer)
- [ ] Good travel insurance: I recommend the one from WorldNomads

Steve Hänisch

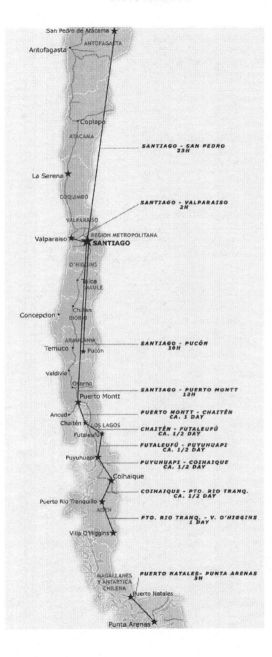

2 MAP & ITINERARIES

All spots described within the guide are highlighted on this map. Furthermore, I added the travel times by bus/car.

The distances are far as the shape of the country is very long and narrow. Ensure that you take some time drafting your own itinerary if your time is limited and you want to see as much as possible.

Especially on the Carretera Austral (Puerto Montt - Villa O'Higgins), the travel times are hard to calculate as there are many ferry crossings and the condition of the road varies considerably.

With this map and the following itinerary suggestions, you can plan several trip options.

As a quick example, I did the tour:
Santiago - San Pedro - Santiago - Concepcion - Pucón - Concepcion - Valparaiso - Santiago during my first time in Chile. It took me three weeks.

On my second trip, I spent the same amount of time only to travel the Carretera Austral.

Especially when you're heading for hiking trips to Patagonia, I encourage you to take the time this region deserves!

If you're short on time, I recommend flying these routes:

Santiago - Calama
Santiago - Puerto Montt
Santiago - Coyhaique and
Santiago - Punta Arenas

My Itinerary Suggestions

Only a few people are able to travel without a time limit as I did. This is why I put together the following itinerary suggestions in which I used the typical vacation time limits of 2-3 weeks as a base (coming from a European standpoint).

You are free to adjust those itineraries to your own liking depending on your individual interests and your time limitations.

In general, I suggest more time for Patagonia because the weather there is unpredictable. Planning a trip along the beautiful Carretera Austral without your own car/rental car is difficult, as public transportation is limited and sometimes quickly sold out.

If you have more than three weeks to spend, you can combine the itineraries.

When you plan flights, keep in mind that domestic flights are always cheaper than international flights e.g. to/from Argentina. The same goes for flights from Argentina to Chile.

Personally, I prefer slow travel and try to minimize flights as much as possible (when you experience Patagonia and its declining glaciers you'll understand why). This is why I covered most of the distances by bus or hitchhiking. I included bus travel times and bus companies in the itineraries to make it easier for you.

Find all information on where to sleep, eat, and what to do within the related travel guides for each spot (3rd chapter).

(A) Volcanoes, Coast & Desert in 2 or 3 Weeks

(Santiago - Pucon - San Pedro de Atacama - Valparaiso - Santiago)

On this trip, you'll experience the wide variety of the country without being in a hurry as you spend several days at each destination.

This itinerary is the exact copy of my first Chile trip (except the fact that I visited friends in Concepcion). I covered all distances by bus and mostly used TurBus to do so.

Be prepared for long distances and huge contrasts in the weather. This is why you should pack accordingly and might consider taking 1-2 domestic flights.

Also, shortening your stay to two weeks isn't a problem, as we will use Santiago as the central hub. You can easily drop one of the three destinations (Valparaiso, Pucon, or San Pedro de Atacama).

Day 1 & 2: Arrival in Santiago (optional)

You'll almost always arrive at the Arturo Benitez airport in Santiago if arriving from abroad. After a long journey, I always recommend a short stopover in the capital to relax and get things started smoothly.

My recommendation is to book an Airbnb or a hostel in Bellavista—a neighborhood famous for its vibe, nightlife, and good restaurants, which is located right in the city center. From here, you can also get to the top of Cerro San Cristobal.

Find more tips and information in the Santiago guide in the travel guide section.

Day 3: Santiago - Pucón (travel day)

Today, you are heading south. Book an early bus that goes directly to Pucón. The journey takes about eleven hours. Therefore, I recommend getting a ticket for the comfortable "cama" class (about 24 USD). You'll arrive in Pucón in the evening.

Alternatively, you can take a plane to Temuco (1.5h) and take the bus from there to Pucón (2h). With "Sky", you can get tickets starting at 40 USD. The additional bus ride is usually about 7 USD

Day 4: Pucón, Planning & Hot Springs

After all those travel days, you should use the first day to plan out your next four days by looking at the weather forecast. You should prioritize the tour to the volcano Villarrica. Consult a good tour operator in town about the best day to do this specific tour and adjust your program accordingly.

Use the rest of your day to explore Pucón. Relax by the lake and go for a tour to the hot springs in the afternoon.

Day 5: Pucón, Huerquehue National Park

The Huerquehue National Park is located just a short drive from Pucón and is an excellent hiking area. Take a look at the various trail options in Pucón and go for a day hike or even a two-day hike. Depending on your choice, you should rent the equipment needed if you don't have it with you.

Day 6: Pucón, Huerquehue National Park or El Cani

Depending on the plan you made the previous day, you could also head to one of my insider tips for the region: the private El Cani park.

Find more information in the Pucón travel guide.

Day 7: Pucón, Volcano Villarrica

The hike to the top of the active volcano Villarrica is the highlight in Pucón. You should have a certain fitness level and go with a local guide.

Please keep in mind that this tour is only doable if the weather is stable. Make sure to have an alternative plan in case of bad luck.

Day 8: Pucón (leisure/buffer)

Use your last days to relax or tackle another outdoor activity.

Day 9: Pucón - Valparaiso (travel day)

Today, you'll have a long travel day ahead as you go back north. Your destination, Valparaiso, is just a two-hour drive from the capital. This is why you first need to travel to Santiago.

Again, you could consider taking a flight for part of the journey (Temuco-Santiago). Tickets are available starting at 45 USD.

Day 10: Valparaiso, Cerros

Use your first day in Valparaiso to explore. Walk up the many cerros (hills) or use one of the "ascensores" (funiculars)

Day 11: Valparaiso, Vina del Mar

It's time for a trip to the long beaches of Vina del Mar, which is just a thirty-minute drive from "Valpo".

Day 12: Valparaiso, House of Pablo Neruda / Departure

If you haven't already done so, you should use this day to discover Valparaiso's street art and pay a visit to the former residence of Pablo Neruda. The house of the famous writer was turned into a museum and offers one of the best views of the city!

If you like, you can also go for a harbor boat trip in the afternoon.

In case you want to cover the next stretch to San Pedro de Atacama by bus, you'd need to leave "Valpo" in the late afternoon.

Day 13: Valparaiso - San Pedro (travel day)

We're heading north. The journey takes about 25 hours by bus. Therefore, you should book "cama" (approx. 60 USD) as you spend the night before and this day on the bus.

If you choose to take a plane, you'll need to go to Santiago first (2h) and take a flight to Calama (2h). From Calama, you can take a bus to get to San Pedro de Atacama (1.5h). The budget airline, Sky, also offers this route starting from 45 USD.

Day 14: San Pedro, Valle de la Luna & Sandboarding

Welcome to the desert! To escape the heat, you should get up early and use the morning hours.

Explore the village and its stores. Use today to plan your stay and browse through the offers of the local tour operators. Find my recommendations in the related travel guide.

Book your first excursion for the late afternoon. Consider sandboarding and the sunset in Valle de la Luna to start your time in San Pedro right!

Day 15: San Pedro, El Tatio Geyser

Today, you need to get up early to see the Tatio Geyser at sunrise—it's a unique experience!

Day 16: San Pedro

Use this day to explore the lagoons and salt flats around San Pedro—I recommend a full day tour.

Alternatively, you can rent bikes and do it on your own. However, be aware of the heat: take enough water, sunscreen, and start early!

Day 17: San Pedro

The last day is for relaxation. Take in the atmosphere and special vibe of San Pedro once more and book a night sky observation tour for tonight—the right way to finish this trip!

Day 18: San Pedro - Santiago (travel day)

Head back to Santiago by bus (arrival in the morning of the next day) or by plane (arrival in the afternoon).

Day 19 & 20: Santiago (optional)

You still have two days to spare. You can these to experience more of the Chilean culture, cuisine, and visit some sights before heading back home.

Day 21: Santiago - Home (travel day)

After an exciting trip through Chile, it is time to head back home. I hope you had a great time!

Notes:

(B) Carretera Austral in 2 or 3 Weeks

(Puerto Montt - Chaitén - Futaleufú - Puyuhuapi - Coyhaique)

or

(Puerto Montt - Chaitén - Futaleufú - Puyuhuapi - Coyhaique - Cerro Castillo - Puerto Río Tranquilo - Coyhaique)

The Carretera Austral is by far the most pristine route of Patagonia. This region is still off the beaten path and the landscape is incredible.

This itinerary takes you to the highlights in the northern section of the Ruta 7. If you have four weeks, it takes you even further south.

The schedule for this trip is activity-filled: you'll hike a lot and raft down the most beautiful rivers in the world. However, be aware of the fact that you need to cover long distances by car on gravel roads to get to your destination (the main reason mass tourism isn't down there yet). The views you'll get to see are all worth it!

To keep up with the schedule, rent a good car (a 4x4 is best) in Puerto Montt that you will take down to Coyhaique where you'll return it. The public buses are sold out quickly during high season and via hitchhiking; it is hard to plan a trip if your time is limited. Chances are you will get stuck in one place for a few days.

First, I'll line out the two-week itinerary. The additional week can be added (you need to switch to the other one on day 12 if you plan on doing the longer version).

Please book your activities and tours in advance, e.g. rafting in Futaleufú, to ensure you get to do all the activities.

Day 1: Arrival in Puerto Montt

Via Santiago de Chile, you'll fly into Puerto Montt, which is the starting point for this trip.

As Puerto Montt isn't the most beautiful city in Chile, consider staying in the nearby Puerto Varas, which is beautifully located next to a lake with a view of the Osorno Volcano.

Day 2: Puerto Montt, Supply Shopping & Puerto Varas

To recover from the long trip to Chile, I recommend a smooth start and using the first day to pick up your car and buy all the supplies needed for your trip. Take plenty of Chilean Peso with you. ATMs are very rare along the Carretera. The same goes for gas stations.

Head also to the tourist information in Puerto Montt where you get all the info needed for ferries and sights as well as free detailed maps of the route.

Use the rest of the day to explore Puerto Varas and its surroundings.

Day 3: Puerto Montt - Chaitén

And off we go! Start early in the morning to make it to the ferry on time. You have three ferry crossings ahead as you take the Ruta 7 (there is also a direct ferry to Chaitén from Puerto Montt). If you're on time for the first ferry, you can simply go with the flow afterward as the ferries are coordinated.

You'll spend most of the day on the ferries floating through the impressive fjord region and arrive in Chaitén in the afternoon.

Day 4: Chaitén, Volcano

On your first day, you should do the short hike to the Chaitén volcano.

Day 5: Chaitén, Pumalin

Today, you can either drive to Pumalin Park and do a few hikes there on your own or book a tour with the lovely people from NaTour (check the Chaitén travel guide).

Day 6: Chaitén - Futaleufú & Yelcho Glacier

The Carretera Austral adventure continues. Start as early as possible to have enough time for the hike to the Yelcho Glacier in the morning (17km south of Chaitén en route south). Find more info about this in the Chaitén travel guide.

Continue on to Futaleufú in the afternoon. The route starts to get bad from Villa Santa Lucia as it turns into a gravel road. If you don't arrive too late in Futaleufú, you should use the time to ask for rafting tours at the offices of the several tour operators in town.

Day 7: Futaleufú, Rafting

If you plan on doing a multi-day rafting trip (book well in advance!) you'll start today with your adventure.

In case you only want to do a one-day rafting tour, you can use this day to check the offers of the several tour operators in town and book your trip for the next day.

Day 8: Futaleufú, Rafting

Enjoy the rapids!

Day 9: Futaleufú - Puyuhuapi

Again, you start in the morning and make your way back to Villa Santa Lucia. From there, you take the Carretera Austral further south until you arrive in the picturesque village of Puyuhuapi (gas station en route in the town of La Junta).

Use the afternoon to walk along the shore and head up to the lookout point to enjoy the sunset over the Bay from there.

Day 10: Puyuhuapi, Queulat Glacier

A very early start is important today in order to have the Queulat National Park almost to yourself. After arrival, head straight to the trail that takes you to the lookout point. This way you avoid the tourist groups and can enjoy a phenomenal view of the Queulat Glacier!

Make sure to also explore the rest of the park and return to Puyuhuapi in the afternoon. If you feel like it, you can also visit the hot springs near Puyuhuapi.

Day 11: Puyuhuapi - Coyhaique, Bosque Encantado

One of the most beautiful parts of the route is waiting for you today. To avoid having a day where you only sit in the car, you should start early.

This time, you drive past the first part of the Queulat National Park (the glacier you visited yesterday) and head south to the second part called "Bosque Encantado". The entrance is located about 20-25km from the first part (see more information inside the Puyuhuapi travel guide). Make a break and take on the short hike to the lagoon.

Around lunchtime/early afternoon, you should be on the road again. On the way to Coyhaique, you should stop as much as possible at the several lookout points along the way. Before you reach Coyhaique, you should make a stop on one of the hills along the route from where you can see the whole city with the mountains in the back.

Day 12: Coyhaique, Cerro Castillo (switch itinerary here if you plan for 3 weeks!)

It's another very early start in order to take on another beautiful day hike—you'll be back in town in the evening.

Drive to Villa Cerro Castillo to do the day trek to Cerro Castillo. You can find parking next to the tiny info point/park ranger hut. Try to start your hike by 10 a.m.!

Day 13: Coyhaique, relaxation (optional)

The last day is for relaxation before you head back home. If you feel like being active, you can go for another sightseeing or hiking trip in the area. Visit the tourist information center in town (near Plaza de Armas) to get good recommendations for the season you are visiting.

Day 14: Departure

After two intense but beautiful weeks, you are heading back home. Have a safe journey!

3-Week-Version

Day 12: Coyhaique, Supply Shopping & Drive to Villa Cerro Castillo

As you are facing a four-day trek you should head into town, buy all the supplies needed and, in case you need some outdoor equipment, use the chance to buy it in Coyhaique (the town has a good number of outdoor shops). In the tourist information center, you can grab some additional maps and valuable information.

Head down to Villa Cerro Castillo in the afternoon.

Day 13-16: Villa Cerro Castillo, Las Horquetas-Cerro Castillo Hike

The starting point is called "Horquetas Grandes" and is located between Coyhaique and Villa Cerro Castillo. You'll finish the trek in Villa Cerro Castillo.

Park your car in Villa Cerro Castillo and try to book a transfer from Villa Cerro Castillo in advance to the starting point of the trek (alternatively, you can hitchhike).

Find more info about the trek in the Villa Cerro Castillo travel guide.

Day 17: Villa Cerro Castillo - Puerto Rio Tranquilo

Today, you keep going south to Puerto Rio Tranquilo. Here, the last stretch is the most picturesque one as you drive along the turquoise General Carrera lake.

Day 18: Puerto Rio Tranquilo, Marble Caves & Relaxation

It's time to have a break after those days of getting up early.

Take it easy, sleep in, and browse through the tour packages at the offices of the tour operators in town for the glacier tour to the Exploradores Glacier (active) or the San-Rafael-Glacier (bus and boat tour).

Go for the boat trip to the marble cave in the afternoon (approx. 2h).

Day 19: Puerto Rio Tranquilo, Glacier Hike

Pack your sunglasses and sunscreen, have a good breakfast, and then head to the impressive Patagonian glaciers!

Day 20: Puerto Rio Tranquilo - Coyhaique

Fill your car with gas in town and then head back to Coyhaique where you'll arrive in the afternoon.

Eat dinner at Mama Gaucha in town.

Day 21: Departure

Wow. What an adventure! I hope you enjoyed your trip and time in this part of Chile. I bet by now you know why it is one of my favorite regions in South America.

Notes:

(C) Carretera Austral & Patagonia in 5 Weeks

(Puerto Montt - Chaitén - Futaleufú - Puyuhuapi - Coyhaique - Cerro Castillo - Puerto Rio Tranquilo - Perito Moreno - El Chaltén - El Calafate - Puerto Natales - Punta Arenas)

If you have more time than just two weeks, you can combine the Carretera Austral easily with Southern Patagonia.

For the Argentinean side, you should get my travel guide for Argentina where you'll also find a hiking guide beside information for each place in this region.

Speaking of the detailed program, you can decide if you want to spend more time in El Chaltén (Argentina) or Puerto Natales depending on your fitness/hiking level. As this itinerary is for people with an average fitness level, I left out the very challenging Huemul Circuit in El Chaltén in favor of the W trek in Torres del Paine. If you wish to do the more extreme version, I recommend you to combine this itinerary with "the Best of Patagonia for Trekking Pro's" itinerary.

Ensure you rent a car that you are allowed to take into Argentina as well!

For the first part of the route, you should follow the "Carretera Austral in 3 weeks (B)" itinerary till day 19. Afterward, you continue with this itinerary:

Day 20: Puerto Rio Tranquilo - Perito Moreno (Argentina)

Fuel up in town and then head for Perito Moreno in Argentina.

The duration of this trip should be approx. five hours. Therefore, you could have some sightseeing stops on the way e.g. in Puerto Guadal and Chilo Chico.

Day 21: Perito Moreno - El Chaltén (Argentina)

Another long drive ahead: until you arrive in El Chaltén, you need to spend approximately eight hours on the road.

Day 22: El Chaltén, Cerro Torre Hike

Time for the first hike. The trek to the Laguna Torre is a long one; however, it is mostly pretty smooth. It is a good way to start your time in El Chaltén.

(Find more information in the Argentina travel guide.)

Day 23: El Chaltén, Fitz Roy Hike

This hike is a bit more challenging, especially the last part of it. Start as early as possible to avoid the tourist groups.

(Find more information in the Argentina travel guide.)

Day 24: El Chaltén

Depending on your energy level, you can have a relaxed day or go for another hike, e.g. to the Tumbado.

ALTERNATIVE Day 22-24: Circuit Trail El Chaltén – Fitz Roy – Cerro Torre

If you prefer to do a multi-day trek, you can also combine the previously mentioned hike and camp out.

(Find more information in the Argentina travel guide.)

Day 25: El Chaltén - El Calafate & Perito Moreno

Get up early to make it to El Calafate with enough time left to see the Perito-Moreno-Glacier.

After 3.5 hours of driving, you will arrive in Calafate.

Check in to your hotel and try to be on the road to the glacier by around lunch time latest. If you wish, you can book a boat tour and/or an ice hike in advance (find more information in the Argentina travel guide).

Day 26: El Calafate - Puerto Natales (travel day)

Time to go back to Chile! After a four-hour drive, you'll arrive in Puerto Natales.

Day 27: Puerto Natales, Shopping & Relaxation

Use today to go grocery shopping for the W Trek. Depending on the season, you should have reserved all your camping sites well in advance (paid and free ones).

Find more in-depth information in the Torres del Paine hiking guide!

Day 28-32: W-Hike, Torres del Paine

The best way to experience this part of Patagonia is through hiking. Find all information needed on preparation, route, equipment, camps, costs, and personal tips in the Torres del Paine hiking guide!

Day 33: Puerto Natales (relaxation, optional)

After five days of hiking, you can use this day to charge up or you can visit the nearby caves.

Day 34: Puerto Natales - Punta Arenas

The last stretch of your trip takes you to Punta Arenas

(approx. three hours of driving). Return your car and reflect on all your experiences while walking along the promenade next to the Strait of Magellan.

Take the boat to see the penguins on Isla Magdalena in the afternoon.

Day 35: Punta Arenas - Santiago - Home

What an incredible month! Have a safe journey back home.

(D) Best of Patagonia for Trekking-Pro's - 3 Weeks

(Torres del Paine Circuit, Chile - Perito Moreno, El Calafate - El Chaltén)

If you are an experienced hiker and want to experience Patagonia in the most active way possible, this is the right itinerary for you.

However, beware. You should only take on this itinerary and its hikes if you are physically fit. You'll have several multi-day hikes within only three weeks; the Huemul Circuit is an especially challenging one.

Please bear in mind that I optimized this itinerary in order to fit as many experiences possible into the given timeframe. I'd usually recommend having more time (four weeks) as the weather is often unpredictable and makes it sometimes impossible and dangerous to hike. By having more time, you'd also have some days in between to recover.

Depending on your fitness level, you should consider skipping some of the hikes in between the multi-day treks.

For the Argentina section, I recommend reading through my Argentina travel guide.

Day 1: Santiago - Punta Arenas (travel day)

To save as much time as possible, head straight down to Patagonia.

Day 2: Punta Arenas - Puerto Natales (travel day)

The journey continues with a bus to Puerto Natales. The drive takes about three hours.

Day 3: Puerto Natales

Use this day to buy everything you need for the circuit hike. Ensure you have all your camps booked in advance, especially during high season. Find more information in the Torres del Paine hiking guide!

Day 4: Puerto Natales (Buffer, optional)

This day is a tiny buffer, just in case the weather is too bad, you arrived late the day before, you still need to do grocery shopping, or you need to rent/buy gear.

Day 5-12: "O" Circuit Hike, Torres del Paine

The best way to experience nature in the park is by hiking.

Find all information needed on preparation, route, equipment, camps, costs, and personal tips in the Torres del Paine hiking guide!

Day 13: Puerto Natales (Regeneration, optional)

After eight days of hiking, you can use this day to charge up or you can visit the nearby caves.

Day 14: Puerto Natales - El Calafate (travel day)

Take the earliest bus possible to El Calafate. After arrival, you should book a tour to the Perito Moreno Glacier. If you'd like to do it without a guide, check the bus schedule.

Find the different options inside the travel guide for Calafate.

Day 15: El Calafate, Perito Moreno - El Chaltén

One of Patagonia's highlights is waiting for you today: the Perito Moreno glacier.

Take the bus to El Chaltén in the afternoon; the drive takes about 2.5-3 hours.

Day 16: El Chaltén, Hike to Fitz Roy

This hike is a bit more challenging, especially the last part of it. Start as early as possible to avoid the tourist groups.

(Find more information in the Argentina travel guide.)

Day 17: El Chaltén, Cerro Torre hike or Relaxation

This is a long hike; however, it is less challenging than yesterday.

Alternatively, you can skip this hike and relax instead to charge up for the toughest hike that is starting tomorrow. Please keep in mind that you need a harness and carabiner in order to do that hike.

Day 18-21: Huemul Circuit

For me, this is one of the most beautiful but challenging treks in Patagonia.

Day 22: El Chaltèn - El Calafate - Buenos Aires - Home (travel day)

The buses from El Chaltén to El Calafate usually stop at the airport. From there, you can fly to Buenos Aires starting at 140 USD (with Aerolineas Argentinas) in about three hours.

You can add some more days to explore Buenos Aires or you

can head straight back home (for this, you most likely need to get a transfer to the international airport Ezeiza).

I hope you enjoyed this very active trip!

3 TRAVEL GUIDES

In contrast to popular travel guides, such as Lonely Planet, I give personal recommendations on tours, accommodation, restaurants, and sights in this chapter.

I've been at most places much longer than the usual backpacker and visited some spots even several times.

Often, I followed recommendations of fellow travelers and locals. I want to use this part of the book to share my insights with you. Of course, I only recommend attractions, ho(s)tels, restaurants and activities that are recommendable in my opinion.

Notes:

San Pedro de Atacama

San Pedro de Atacama is the destination if you would like to explore the driest desert in the world. It is located in the very north and awaits you with an amazing landscape defined by volcanos, salt flats, lagoons, and rock formations.

Get In

This region is located in the very north of Chile and stretches to the Bolivian border in the west. The small desert village of San Pedro de Atacama is the perfect base for discoveries in that area.

If you landed in Santiago, the capital of Chile, you have two options to get to San Pedro. The most comfortable (but also expensive) way is to fly to Calama (e.g. with LAN or Sky) and then take the bus for the last 100km. The most popular option is to take one of the very comfortable long distance buses to the north; for around 35 USD, you can book a seat in semi-cama (half bed) for the 1700km and journey time of 23 hours (you'll have 30min stops every five hours).

If you want to travel from Bolivia, the best option is to end your Uyuni Tour at the border. From there, you can take organized transfers to San Pedro (mostly bookable with the tour companies in Uyuni).

Things to See & Do

✦ San Pedro de Atacama & Salt flats

The village is the touristic center of the region. Therefore, you'll find a lot of hostels, restaurants, and tour agencies around. During the day, San Pedro is a quiet place as there is not much to see or do in the village itself (apart from the church).

As a result of the fact that San Pedro is located in the Atacama Desert, you should consider that the temperatures in the night are dropping extremely (in September it is around 30 degrees at daytime and around -5 in the night).

The Salar de Atacama is located right next to San Pedro and is the largest salt flat in the country. If you'd like to be active, you can rent mountain bikes. Please consider taking enough water and sunscreen with you and try to start your tour early in the morning!

✦ The Moon valley

The "Valle de la Luna" is a MUST DO. You can see impressive rock formations, caves, and colors. The best time to experience it is before/during sunset.

The common tours always start in the afternoon with several stops where you get to see the highlights and will get to know more about the geological history. At the end of the tour, you'll enjoy the sunset from one of the many viewpoints.

I decided to book all my tours in the office of "Cactus" (on the main street) and highly recommend that you do this, too. They have really good guides with the right sense of humor, serve delicious food on long tours, and usually have small groups. However, the tours are a little bit more expensive (for me it was worth it).

✦ Sandboarding

In search of some action? Then you have to book the sandboarding trip directly at the office of the tour operator organizing that adventure (just watch out for sandboarding pictures and sandboards at the entrance - don't book in one of the offices of the big tour agencies who only refer and take an additional fee from you). You'll drive to a big sand dune with a group of mostly young people and slide down that dune for a few hours after a short briefing. Bring enough water and sunscreen with you (there is no lift/elevator; you have to walk up the dune).

After around two hours, you'll go on a small tour through Moon Valley and will finish the trip by having pisco/beer at a lookout spot while watching the sunset.

A great option to connect the Moon Valley tour with some fun stuff!

✦ Lagoons & Salt Flat

The area around the salt flat is full of contrasts. Here, you can see flamingos, volcanoes, and colorful lagoons. The full-day lagoon tour covers mostly the salt flat, Laguna Miscanti, and Laguna Miniques with a stop at Toconao.

This tour starts early in the morning and you'll have breakfast right next to the numerous flamingos at the salt flat before heading to the lagoons.

✦ Tatio Geysers and Cactus Valley

The geysers at the foot of the El Tatio volcano are the world's third largest, containing 8% of all geysers to be found on our planet.

Definitely a MUST do: you start very early in the morning (4 am) to arrive at the highest geothermal field in the world right on time for the sunrise. In the beginning, it is freezing cold (we had around -10 degrees Celsius) but the whole area is stunning. Because of the low temperatures, you see the smoke coming out of the geysers. After sunrise, it gets warm really quickly.

Use your chance to jump in one of the hot springs (the water temperature is around 30 degrees).

Some tour operators also add a stop at the cactus valley to the trip. Ask for the exact itinerary before you book and compare the services offered (we had a full board tour including breakfast and two additional stops).

✦ Observation of the Night Sky

There is a reason why the world's largest telescopes are to be found here. You won't find clouds and the density is really low resulting in very low light pollution.

You can find two operators in San Pedro offering observation tours of the night sky where you'll learn a lot and have the chance to see planets and stars through several telescopes set up in the desert. I've never seen planets so clearly or so detailed!

Restaurants / Cafés / Bars

Cafe Esquina

If you want to eat healthily, this is the right spot: tasty sandwiches, vegetarian dishes, salads, & freshly squeezed juices.

Though it is more expensive, it is worth it. It is one of the best (if not the best) option for a good breakfast!

Restaurant Barros --- set menu 5 USD

A place that is well-known and offers the best value for money with set menus for only 5 USD.

At night, it's a good place for drinks and live music!

Accommodation in San Pedro

On my last trip to San Pedro, I chose the Hostal Rural—one of the most popular hostels for a reason. They have four-bed and six-bed dorms, a relaxed atmosphere, and a good location off the main street.

You can find the link to book this hostel and an overview of options in San Pedro inside the link list I provided.

Where to go next

Santiago   - 23 hrs   (Operator: TurBus)

Salta (Argentinien) - 11 hrs   (Operator: Andesmar)

Uyuni (Bolivien)   - 3-day Jeep Sightseeing Tour

To get into Bolivia & Peru:

Calama   - 1 h

Arica   - 10 hrs

Notes:

Santiago

Like in most of the other countries in South America, nearly 40% of the people live in the capital. In Santiago, it is around seven out of 17 million.

The special thing about Chile's capital is that it is located directly next to the Andes—you can see them if it is not too misty.

Get In

Santiago is mostly the starting point for backpacking in Chile or even a big South America trip because the airport, "Arturo Merino Benitez", is a big hub within the continent.

The same goes for bus connections as all national and many international long-distance bus routes come together in the Chilean capital. If you are arriving from Argentina you'll most likely use the route from Mendoza.

When arriving by plane, you should be aware that the airport is located outside the city. It is highly recommended that you use one of the collectivos (shared taxis service in mini bus or vans). The best companies are "TransVIP" and "TransCity". Their representatives can be found at the airport (often at the baggage claim).

Things to See & Do

✦ Plaza de Armas & Museum

The city center feels a bit like walking around in a city in Spain. Go for a walk through the heart of the capital to the Plaza de Armas and consider visiting the national museum "Museo de Bellas Artes".

✦ Barrio Bellavista

This district is located right next to the old town and is known as the Bohéme area where you can go for a good night out.

At daytime, the walk up to the „Cerro Bellavista" is worth the effort as you can see the inner city as well as the Andes from there on a clear day.

✦ Cerro San Cristobal

The largest hill within the city is a MUST for every tourist.

Take the cable car up there and enjoy the most incredible views of Santiago!

Accommodation in Santiago

The Bellavista Hostel is the most popular option for backpackers and is perfectly located right in Bellavista. You can book 4/6 bed dorms and private rooms (double or single).

If you are searching for a private room, the best option is to rent an Airbnb as you get great value for the money spent. On my last trip, I rented a whole flat on the top floor of a skyscraper with an exceptional view over the city for the price of a regular hotel room.

You can find the link to book this hostel and an overview of options in Santiago inside the link list I provided - here you can also get a discount of 38 USD for your first booking on Airbnb by using my link!

Get Out

San Pedro de Atacama	- 23 hrs	
Pucón	- 10 hrs	
Mendoza (Argentinien)	- 8 hrs	(company: Cata)
Buenos Aires	- 21 hrs	(company: Cata)
Puerto Montt	- 13 hrs	

Notes:

Valparaiso & Vina del Mar

With a population of only around 275,000, Valpo (as locals like to call it), is not one of the biggest cities. However, it is well known worldwide. The reason for that? The area in and around Valparaiso with its colorful houses and street art is the cultural center and is home to the country's most important seaport.

Get In

If you intend to travel from Santiago, you can take one of the regular bus connections (several buses every hour). The trip will take a bit less than two hours.

From the bus terminal, I recommend taking a taxi to your accommodation as the terminal is located a bit out of the center.

Things to See & Do

✦ Cerro Concepcion & Cerro Bellavista

If you are going to visit Valparaiso, it's the best to go without any plans. The claim for your visit should be: just walk around and get lost. However, I would definitely recommend having a map with you and inform yourself about the dangerous zones there. If you stay in the center at day, around the Cerros Bellavista and Concepcion should be fine.

Valpo has about 42 cerros/hills that make you use a lot of stairways or the ascensors (elevators, mostly about 100years old). On your way through the town, you will see a lot of street art but there are also many ateliers and art shops. Altogether with its beautiful countryside and the colorful houses, it is not a surprise that the historic and cultural center of Valparaiso is a UNESCO World Cultural Heritage Site.

✦ Pablo Nerudas House

Enjoy the best view from the house of Pablo Neruda. The former residence of the Nobel Prize winner was turned into a lovely museum.

✦ A Trip to Vina del Mar

Vina del Mar is often called the noble suburb of Valparaiso because everything seems to be more organized and clean there.

Vina is located next to Valpo (just 15 minutes by bus). You can find many beautiful beaches with palm trees and beach clubs, parks, and a lively nightlife.

Don't forget to visit "Castillo Wulf"—a museum located next to the beach. There is no entrance fee!

Accommodation in Valparaiso

For your time in Valparaiso I recommend the Hostel Casa Volante which has a great location and you can choose between dorms or private rooms (double/single).

You can find the link to book this hostel and an overview of options in Valparaiso inside the link list I provided.

Restaurants / Cafés / Bars

Head to Cerro Concepcion where you'll find the best restaurants in town. Ensure you ask at the reception for the latest recommendations!

Get Out

La Serena - 7 hrs

Santiago - 1:45 hrs

Pucón   - 12 hrs

Notes:

Pucón

The right destination for outdoor lovers: rafting, hiking, climbing up a volcano, and enjoying hot springs. Pucon is a MUST for active backpackers!

Get In

Though there are flight connections from Santiago to Temuco, the bus is mostly cheaper and there are regular bus connections with TurBus. Overall, the trip takes 9-11 hours.

I took the bus from Concepcion, which took about six hours because I had to change the bus in Temuco with a waiting time of two hours (local operator: BioBio, JAC).

If you are coming from the south, you'll regular connections from Osorno and Puerto Montt. There is also one bus connection to Bariloche in Argentina.

Things to See & Do

I booked all my tours at the hostel, which cooperates with the local agency "Sierra Nevada" (you'll find them opposite from the town hall on the main street of Pucon). The guides here are pretty good, especially for the volcano tour. Highly recommended!

✦ Volcano Villarrica

There is absolutely no question about it: climbing the Volcano Villarrica is a MUST DO if you are in Pucon. The Villaricca Volcano is the second most active volcano in South America and was the main reason for my stay in Pucon.

My plan was to climb the most dangerous volcano in Chile (because of the short distance to Pucon); however, I knew it would be not easy to do. In the agency, our tour group got the stuff needed: climbing boots, crampons, helmet, jacket and pants, backpack, and an icepick. We started at 7 a.m, with the bus and began our walk from the parking space of "Ski Pucon": after an exhausting six-hour hike, we reached the top and enjoyed a breathtaking panoramic view and could even look inside the crater.

Consider that this is a very active volcano and there are no tours if the volcano is erupting. The last big eruption took place on March 9th, 2015. Be sure to check the news before making plans!

✦ Huerquehue Park

Huerquehue Park is one of three national parks around Pucon. The park is a good spot for short and long hikes because you have good signposted paths.

Unfortunately, we had only three hours for a short walk but we made our way along the lake and through the primeval forest to see a huge waterfall and a nice lookout.

I'd recommend taking more time and doing the whole "Three Lakes Hiking Trail."

✦ **Hiking / Snowshoeing in El Cani**

The region around Pucon is called the Araucania Region because of the trees you can find here. The Araucaria tree is one of the oldest trees of the world and the national tree of Chile. Many of these trees can be seen in the private national park "El Cani": a park that was founded by some local people who wanted to protect the area from the woodworking industry, so they bought the territory.

El Cani is a phrase from the Mapuche language and can be translated as "the changing view". If you are on top of this high plateau, you'll realize what this phrase means.

You can only visit the park if you hire a private guide. Moreover, there aren't any marks or signs, which makes it necessary to have a local guide with you. If it's snowy you'll be equipped with snowshoes to discover the former crater of a volcano (the path up there is pretty steep and exhausting!).

✦ **Hot Springs**

In this area, you'll find many hot springs because of the volcanic activities in the region. I highly recommend booking a trip right after your trekking tour to the top of the Villarrica volcano.

I booked this trip at my hostel and it was well organized, including a pickup right from the hostel for a good overall price.

Accommodation in Pucón

After numerous recommendations from friends and other backpackers, I decided to stay at the Hostel „El Refugio" and was very happy with that choice!

The hostel has a great common area with a chimney and helps you to organize your trips—be it to the volcano, rafting, or to the nearby hot springs.

It is also suitable for couples as there are nice private rooms.

You can find the link to book this hostel and an overview of options in Pucón inside the link list I provided.

Get Out

Temuco   - 2 hrs
(Big bus hub in that area with connections to Argentina)

Santiago   - 10 hrs

Valparaiso   - 12 hrs

Puerto Varas & Puerto Montt

Puerto Montt can be described as the gateway to Patagonia and the starting point for adventures on the Carretera Austral while Puerto Varas offers the opportunity to climb a volcano and awaits you with some good German cake. Hmmm. Black forest cake!

Get in

Puerto Montt is the larger city and can be reached by air (airport El Tepual) or by bus. As a result of its importance, there are many connections to the north and to Argentina.

Another possibility is the port if you are coming from the south. The Navimag ferry is the most popular regular connection to Puerto Natales with a stopover in Puerto Chacabuco.

Between Puerto Montt and Puerto Varas, you can find many regular connections. The travel time is about 30-40 minutes.

Things to See & Do

✦ Puerto Varas

Other than Puerto Montt, this small town is located right at the lake Llanquihue and is very picturesque.

Beside a stroll through the town, which has been founded by German settlers, I recommend visiting the church (which is meant to be a copy from a church in the Black forest), the promenade at the lake, and the hike up the small hill next to the lake.

Did I mention the cake? Don't miss out treating yourself at one of the cafés in town!

✦ Pablo Fierro Museum, Puerto Varas

This one-of-a-kind museum is located right on the street that runs along the promenade (coming from the city center, you have to go right).

Pablo Fierro is an artist who originally did restoration work on old houses and started collecting many things he came across while doing jobs. He decided to display those items and opened up his own museum full of interesting stuff.

When his car—a Volkswagen—is parked in front of the house, he is at the museum awaiting curious guests. The whole experience is free. Mostly, he will show you around and tell his many stories. A true character! If you feel like, you can donate some money to help him keep the museum going.

✦ Kayaking, Hiking, Rafting

If this is relevant to your interests, you'll find many tour operators offering tours in the city center of Puerto Vargas (I didn't go for this as I had done it in Patagonia already).

✦ Osorno Volcano & Salto Petrohué

The shape of this volcano reminded me very much to Mount Fuji in Japan, especially when you take a picture standing on the shore of the lake in Puerto Varas.

Unlike the Villarrica volcano, you can drive almost all the way up to the top: the road ends at a viewpoint (at 1300m) where you can have a drink at the restaurant and even hit the slopes in wintertime—a chairlift brings you closer to the top of the mountain. When making your way back down, you should head to the Waterfall "Saltos de Petrohué", which is worth the small entrance fee.

✦ Chiloé

Unfortunately, I never got to visit Chiloé on my numerous trips to the region but I had a lot of chats with locals and travelers who have been there, which have persuaded me to pay it a decent visit when I'm back.

On the matter of natural beauty and location, this island definitely deserves a multi-day visit!

Restaurants / Cafés / Bars in Puerto Varas

✦ Restaurant Tomacito

Hearty Chilean cuisine for good prices - open until 9 p.m.
Cazuela from 5 USD // Chorillana 7.5 USD

✦ Café Puerto

Snacks, good beer, and friendly service.
My recommendation: Pichanga for 15 USD

◆ **La Barrista**

Best coffee in town and a good atmosphere.

◆ **Pim's Pub**

Though the food is a bit pricey, you should head there and try their beer!

◆ **Café at the Promenade / Plaza**

Here, you'll get very good cake and you'll have one of the best views of the lake and the volcano from the rooftop terrace.

Accommodation in Puerto Varas

I stayed at the Puerto Varas Hostel right in the center and close to the lake. The hostel offers dorms as well as private rooms.

Although the prices in Puerto Varas are comparably high, you get good value as the breakfast is rich and good!

Further, the staff working here is nice and helpful. The hostel offers tours that can be booked at the reception as well.

Accommodation in Puerto Montt

As mentioned, I don't recommend staying in Puerto Montt. However, sometimes it's better e.g. if you need to catch the Navimag ferry or if you're planning to travel along the Carretera Austral.

I stayed at the Rocco Casa Hostel for one night, which is located close to the bus terminal and the harbor—nice staff and good rooms!

You can find the link to book these hostels and an overview of options in Puerto Varas & Puerto Montt inside the link list I provided.

Get Out

Santiago — - 13 hrs

Osorno — - 1:30 h

Puerto Natales — - 4 day / 3 nights
(Company: Navimag Ferry)

Bariloche (Arg) — - 6-7 hrs
(Company: Cruz del Sur)

Punta Arenas (flight) — - 2 hrs
(Company: LATAM or Sky Airline)

Notes:

The Carretera Austral (Overview)

Route 7 connects the most remote areas of Chile and is one of the most beautiful roads in South America. It is an alternative road to the Panamericana, which is located on the Argentinean side of Patagonia.

Amongst bikers and cyclists, this route is popular because of the beautiful landscape even though the road was not constructed for tourism purposes. If you intend to go by car, you should make sure you have at least a 4WD because of partially rough road conditions.

Nowadays, the Carretera is a mostly unpaved road and is located in two regions of Chile: Region Los Lagos in the north and Region Aysen in the south.

You'll be rewarded with fjord crossings, glaciers, picturesque valleys, lakes, marble caves, and small, remote fishing villages.

Get In

The Carretera Austral starts in Puerto Montt and finishes in Villa O'Higgins. I traveled it twice: in 2013 I hitchhiked from Villa O'Higgins to Puerto Montt and did so vice versa in 2016.

How you get to Puerto Montt can be found in the previous chapter. If you want to, you can start like me in Villa O'Higgins.

The starting point for trips to Villa O'Higgins is El Chaltén in Argentina where you take a bus to the southern point of the Lago del Desierto. From here, you take a boat to the northern point of the lake where also the Argentinian border checkpoint is located. You have to hike the remaining twelve kilometers to Candelario Mansilla on the Chilean side.

Candelario Mansilla is a farm located on O'Higgins Lake. From here, there is a regular boat connection to Villa O'Higgins during the summer season. You can rent rooms in Candelario Mansilla with breakfast included. You can also opt-in for an excursion to the nearby O'Higgins glacier with the same boat that takes you later to Villa O'Higgins!

Find a detailed itinerary and all information needed about this border crossing in the related trekking guide!

Things to See & Do

The whole road from north to south is breathtaking. I don't know of any better road trip in the world.

After finishing my second trip, I can say I visited almost all the highlights along the Carretera Austral and did my very best to sum it up in the following travel guides.

Ensure you bring some time to enjoy the Ruta 7 to the fullest!

Accommodation

As this is a remote area in South America, you should focus on spending the nights in hospedajes and rooms rented out by locals. The people are very friendly and sometimes even offer home cooked meals for their guests!

Unlike at tourist hot spots, I recommend just going to some hospedajes. Ask for the price and have a look at the interior before you make your decision. This worked out very well for me and I never had a problem finding a place to stay. Moreover, you keep as much flexibility as possible and don't need to plan ahead.

Update (March '17): Be aware that the road sparks more and more interest, so it might be wise to plan a bit ahead for the most popular spots e.g. Puerto Rio Tranquilo & Puyuhuapi.

Transportation

You have the following options to travel along the Carretera Austral:

- Hitchhike
- Bike
- Motorbike
- Local Buses
- Car

As stated, I hitchhiked most of the route and had a blast. However, I highly recommend learning some proper Spanish before (see the options I pointed out in the Preparation chapter).

Having your own car definitely gives you more flexibility in matters of timing and the places you are able to visit. Again, for this, you'd need a proper Jeep because of the rough road conditions. If you plan on renting a camper, you should check out Wicked Campers South America. Here, you can rent the car in Purto Varas and return it in Punta Arenas.

Have in mind to plan much more time than on normal, paved roads!

Chaitén

Chaitén is the first town you get to see along the Carretera Austral coming from the north. Chaitén acts as the gate to this part of Patagonia and gets more popular each year.

Get In

When you take the Carretera Austral, you'll need to take altogether three ferries to get here. The whole trip takes about one full day.
There is also a regular bus connection with "Kemel Bus" for about 22USD.

Another option is the direct ferry connection from Puerto Montt (12 hrs, 2-3 times per week) or from Chiloé (4 hrs, only on certain days).

The third option would be coming from the south: the tiny village of Santa Lucia is 75km down the road (1.5 hrs), La Junta about 144km (3 hrs).

Things to See & Do

✦ Fjord crossing Puerto Montt - Chaitén

The first highlight is actually the route to Chaitén. You can choose to take the ferry or to go by car or bus. If you go by car or bus, you'll have three picturesque ferry crossings along the way, which remind you of the landscape in Norway.

Before you embark on your journey, you should go to the tourist information in Puerto Montt where you can get a map with the schedules of all ferries along the whole Carretera Austral.

✦ Chaitén

A few years ago, this town was destroyed by a volcano and is now in the stage of getting reconstructed slowly. You can still see the affect the catastrophe had when you go for a walk around town; luckily, nobody was killed, as the government evacuated the city on time.

✦ Pumalin Park

The Pumalin Park is located between Hornopiren and Chaitén. The Pumalin Park is one of the first conservation projects by the American, Douglas Thompkins (founder of The North Face), who bought particularly large areas in the region to put them under protection.

The landscape and the fauna in this temperate rainforest are impressive. Inside the park, there are several things to see along with campgrounds and marked trails.

The park's website has all the information needed, including trail descriptions (see link list). There is free admission to the park!

Backpacking in Chile

✦ Chaitén Volcano

This short hike leads you to the crater of the Chaitén volcano. The trail is well marked and only 4.5km but has an elevation of 600m. To get to the starting point of the hike, you first need to drive 24km out of Chaitén heading north.

All information needed can be found online (see link list).

✦ Yelcho Glacier

About 17km south of Chaitén, you have the chance to get to see your first glacier along the Carretera Austral by tackling a 3-4 hour hike. The trail starts about 2 km after you pass Puerto Cardenas, right behind the bridge on the left-hand side (coming from the north).

✦ Futaleufú (150km drive, junction in Villa Santa Lucia)

The reason this is a long drive is worth it: the Futaleufú River, which is often referred to as one of the best white water rafting spots in the world. The landscape along the river is unique and, because of its location, it's still pretty much untouched.

For rafting and kayaking expeditions, I recommend ExChile. I have been on a two-day rafting tour with Chris and his guides and it has been great: the camp as well as the guides. We had a lot of fun!

Restaurants / Cafés / Bars

✦ Natour Food Truck

This food truck can be found in the center of Chaitén and is the project of a young Chilean-German couple.

After they were searching for a place to open a restaurant, they simply decided to convert an old bus.

Beside good German cake, drinks, and completos (hot dogs), NaTour is also a tour operator offering some cool excursions in the area. The staff here is friendly and can also help you out if you need some tips or help with planning your trip. Highly recommended!

Address: Calle Libertador Bernardo O'Higgins

✦ **Pizzeria Reconquista**

Tasty homemade pizza and a good selection of local brews (go for the Cerveza Austral!). You might need to have some patience in high season but it is worth it!

Adsress: Diego Portales 269

Accommodation in Chaitén

The lovely owner of my hostel in Puerto Montt (Casa Rocco) was so kind to call a friend of her who owns the "Hosteria Llanos" to reserve a double room for me and my friend.

I can highly recommend this option. We paid about 45 USD for two people, including breakfast.

As Chaitén can be quite busy during high season (it's a popular destination amongst Chileans), you should consider making a reservation. (Spanish only)

Email: hosteriallanos@yahoo.cl; Tel: 56652731332

Backpacking in Chile

Get out

Villa Santa Lucia	- ca. 1,5 hRS
Futaleufú	- ca. 4hrs (Bus: „Cardenas")
La Junta	- ca. 3hrs (Buses Becker)
Puyuhuapi	- ca. 4hrs (Buses Becker)
Puerto Montt	- ca. 10-12hrs (Kemel Bus)
Quellon (Chiloé)	- ca. 6hrs (ferry)

Notes:

Puyuhuapi

This small village is located on a picturesque bay of the Atlantic Ocean and was founded by German settlers. A great overnight spot that you should use to visit the nearby Queulat National Park and the impressive hanging glacier of Queulat (see picture below)!

Get in

Coming from the north, it only takes about one hour to get here from La Junta. From Chaitén or Futaleufú, it takes around about four hours.

If you are coming from the south, you should plan with at least a five-hour drive from Coyhaique (2/3 of the road is paved).

Things to See & Do

✦ Bay of Puyuhuapi

Puyuhuapi is located on the shores of a bay. There a path that leads along the water (to the right) up to a little viewpoint (you need to go through a gate and follow the marks/signs). After 15 minutes, you will reach a bench where you can enjoy a beautiful view of Puyuhuapi.

✦ Queulat-Glacier, Queulat-National Park (20 km south of Puyuhuapi, entrance fee: 5,000 CLP = 8USD)

The Queulat National Park with its hanging glacier is an absolute Must-See.

Das absolute Must-See ist der Nationalpark Queulat mit seinem hängenden, gleichnamigen Gletscher.

In the Queulat National Park, you can hike to a lookout point that offers the best view of the enormous glacier. Be sure to start your day as early as possible in order to get there before most tourists arrive. Another option to get up close to the glaciers is by boat (5,000 CLP = 8 USD).

If you don't travel by car, you can use a transfer, which is offered in town (ask at the tourist office in Puyuhuapi). Alternatively, try to get there via hitchhiking (which I did).

✦ Bosque Encantado (45km south Puyuhuapi, parking at km 170)

The "enchanted forest" is located on a pass along the Carretera Austral between Puyuhuapi and Coyhaique. It is also part of the Queulat National Park and awaits with a 1.7km trail that leads you to a glacier lagoon through a beautiful forest. Depending on the time of year, it can be covered with ice and snow.

Restaurants / Cafés / Bars

✦ Los Manios del Queulat

This is one of the best restaurants in town with a cozy atmosphere and lovely staff. I had merluza (hake) and tried the steak—both were super delicious and filling.

Address: Circunvalacion S/N

✦ Hosteria Alemana

One of the many family-owned businesses founded by German immigrants. Besides accommodation, you can enjoy homemade cake and coffee here.

Address: Av Otto Uebel

✦ Comuyhuapi

This fairly new place combines a hosteria and restaurant. The ladies offer daily dishes, as well as cake. It is beautifully located with a view of the bay.

Address: Av Otto Uebel

Accommodation in Puyuhuapi

As in many other spots, I did my research after arrival by walking around town and asking at several Hospedajes/Hosterias. Both times I visited Puyuhuapi, I ended up sleeping at the Hosteria "Carretera Austral" right on the main street. The rooms are simple but clean. A double room is 28,000CLP (42 USD) per night, including breakfast.

Other good options you can also reserve in advance via email or telephone are Comuyhuapi, the Hosteria Alemana and Casa Ludwig.

If you want to spoil yourself and enjoy the hot springs at the same time, consider the luxurious Puyuhuapi Lodge & Spa!

You can find the link to book these hostels/hotels and an overview of options in Puyuhuapi inside the link list I provided.

Get out

Coyhaique   - ca. 5hrs (Buses Becker)

La Junta   - ca. 1hrs (Buses Becker)

Chaiten   - ca. 4hrs (Buses Becker)

Puerto Ciscnes - ca. 3hrs

Coyhaique & Cerro Castillo

Coyhaique is located about halfway through the Carretera Austral and is the largest city in this region of Chile. With its airport and budget-friendly flight connections to Santiago & Puerto Montt, the capital of the Aysen region offers a good touristic infrastructure and is a good option to start or end your trip if you run out of time.

Get In

To get straight to Coyhaique, the best option is the nearby airport "Balmaceda" (IATA Code: BBA). You can book flights with LaTam or Sky from Puerto Montt, starting at 25 USD if you book ahead of time.

If you go by car, it takes you about five hours to get here from Puyuhuapi. Coming from the south, it is about 1.5 hours from Villa Cerro Castillo and 5.5 hours from Puerto Rio Tranquilo.

Things to See & Do

Coyhaique is a good spot for a layover. Here, you can stock up on supplies, go for a nice dinner, get some missing outdoor equipment at one of the many outdoor shops, and get some cash from the ATM.

✦ Roadtrip to the North (Maniguales, Reserva Nacional Coyhaique & RN Rio Simpson)

If you didn't get in by car from the north you should take a car and drive this picturesque stretch to Villa Maniguales. The landscape in and around the national parks of Coyhaique and Rio Simpson is just amazing.

On the way back, you have a great view over Coyhaique on a little hill just before you get into town.

✦ Cerro Castillo (nearby Villa Cerro Castillo) - day hike or 4 day hike

The MUST-SEE in this area is located 1.5 hours to the south, close to the tiny village of Villa Cerro Castillo, which is turning more and more into a touristic hot spot. The reason for this is the impressively shaped mountain "Cerro Castillo".

On my first trip, I only passed through but told myself to return and hike up there. In 2016, I took on the day hike up to the Cerro Castillo. The view of the castle-like peaks (hence, the name) and its glacier combined with the front of the glacier is unique—the same applies to the view in the Ibañez River Valley during ascent and descent.

If you have more time, the multi-day circuit hike is one of the most beautiful treks in Patagonia and is a real find! The starting point of the trek is "Horquetas Grandes". You should plan four days for this and be fully equipped (there are only wild camps). You can get corresponding info and tickets in Coyhaique (tourist information center, outdoor shops, guides).

✦ Trekking, Rafting & More

As a result of increased tourism in the past few years, there are new tours and activities being offered each year. To get an overview I highly recommend the very friendly and helpful staff at the local tourist office (Spanish & English speaking!) who are happy to help you planning. Moreover, you can get good maps for free.

Generally speaking, Coyhaique is the center for mountaineers and adventurers alike in the area. This is why you can find many good outdoor shops in the city center, as well as guides who offer their services (ask at the shops).

You can find the tourist office in the Calle Bulnes off the main square Plaza de Armas.

Restaurants / Cafés / Bars

✦ Mama Gaucha in Coyhaique (mains for 10-14 USD)

My favorite restaurant in town! I went there three times during my four-day stay, for a good reason! The homemade pizza, which comes out of a traditional pizza stove and the pasta (especially the one with lamb) are just great and the beer, which comes from a nearby microbrewery, is tasty, too.

Mama Gaucha is also the place to be for travelers and local mountaineers alike. If you stay long in Coyhaique, you'll return more than once!
(I apologize for the lack of more recommendations for Coyhaique but this place was just sooo good!)

Address: Horn 47

✦ **Restaurant Villarrica in Villa Cerro Castillo (mains for 10 USD)**

The only big restaurant in the village offers solid Chilean dishes (meat a lá Pobre with fries)—just about the right thing after a long day of hiking to the Cerro Castillo.

Address: Avenida Bernardo O'Higgins 592

Accommodation in Coyhaique

I went with the locals' recommendations both times I visited the city. On my last visit, I got a good one from the tourist office. Make sure you ask for hosterias that are located in the center.

One place I can particularly recommend is the family-owned Hosteria Monica. For a double room (bathroom ensuite), we paid about 42 USD, including breakfast and Wi-Fi. Address: Calle Eusebio Lillo 664.

Accommodation in Villa Cerro Castillo

On my last trip, I walked around the village and searched for a room by knocking on many doors. Tourism here is still in its early stage.

For camping, I recommend "Patagonia Rustika" (ask for Jorge). You can find the camp at the end of a gravel road that leads to the ranger post and start of the trail from the day hike to the Cerro Castillo (when in doubt, just ask in the village for „campamento de Jorge").

Another place that offers a limited number of rooms is the restaurant Villarrica.

Get Out

Puyuhuapi - ca. 5hrs
(Buses Becker)

Villa Cerro Castillo - ca. 1,5hrs
(Buses Becker, Don Carlos)

Puerto Rio Tranquilo - ca. 5,5hrs
(Buses Becker, Acuario, Sao Paulo)

Puerto Montt (plane) - ca. 1hrs
(Sky, LaTam)

Santiago (plane) - ca. 2,5hrs
(LaTam direct, Sky via Pto. Montt)

Notes:

Puerto Rio Tranquilo

For the next 2-3 days, you should stop in Puerto Rio Tranquilo, which is right on the banks of the second-largest lake in South America. The place is known for its marble caves not far from Puerto Rio Tranquilo but also access to the Northern Patagonian ice field.

Get In

At this stretch of the road, the Carretera Austral is a gravel road that ends up in longer driving times. The easiest way to get in if you only want to visit this place is to drive from the south coming in from Argentina via Chile Chico, but also this route will take up to 4.5 hours of driving.

From Coyhaique and its nearby airport, you'd have about 6 hours of driving.

Things to See & Do

In the center of town, you can find several tour offices right on the main street next to each other opposite the gas station (yes, there is a new gas station in town. Yeah!) and restaurants.

✦ Marble Caves & General Carrera Lake

You should definitely go on a boat excursion to the marble caves "Capillas de Marmol" beneath marble monoliths that extend not far from Puerto Rio Tranquilo. After seeing the photograph at the beginning of this chapter, you should be convinced that it is totally worth it.

I recommend picking Explorasur as your tour operator. The owner, Pato, not only took me on an expedition to the caves. He also gave me a lift when I was hitchhiking to Puerto Rio Tranquillo the day before. Such a great guy! Make sure to say hi from me!

In addition to the caves, the Lago General Carrera itself is true eye candy!

✦ Exploradores-Glacier (approx. 55 USD p.p.)

The second activity you shouldn't miss is the ice hike on the Exploradores glacier in the Laguna San Rafael National Park. For me, it was one of the best glacier experiences along the Carretera Austral.

This one-day tour (starting at about 9 a.m.) requires physical fitness but is well worth the effort. Using crampons, trek across the ice and through impressive glacial caves.

It is hard to find a full-day glacier tour in Patagonia as budget friendly as this one. For the complete package, which includes transportation, guide, equipment, and food, we paid just 55 USD per person!!

✦ Glacier Laguna San Rafael

You can also book excursions to the San Rafael glacier in Puerto Rio Tranquilo. This also involves a longer bus drive to get to the bay where you board a boat that brings you to the glacier.

At this very spot, you can see the undeniable results of global warming. Each year, the boat trip to the glacier gets longer.

Because of its remote location, the San Rafael glacier is not frequented by many tourists in comparison with its more popular "brothers and sisters" in Patagonia. A good reason to visit before it's gone!

Restaurants / Cafés / Bars

Another town where tourism led to a little boom with a massive increase in visitors in the past two years. This is why you can find a fairly high amount of restaurants in comparison to the size of the town. Only Wi-Fi is still hard to get.

✦ Cerveceria (beer from 5 USD)

This brewery recently opened and is one of the best spots in town in matters of good beer—they have three brews on tap. I can recommend the "rojo". The Cerveceria is also a good spot to connect and the food is delicious, too.

During high season, arrive early to get a spot!

Address: Carretera Austral, right next to the gas station

✦ Restaurant Al Paso (Churrasco for 9 USD)

This is the place for typical Chilean cuisine. I can recommend the big Churrascos (huge sandwiches with beef or chicken and a lot of Avocado).

Address: Carretera Austral, also next to the gas station

+ **Hosteria & Restaurant Costanera (Cordero from 14 USD)**

This is the place to try THE local dish of this region: Cordero Patagonico (lamb that is grilled next to an open fire for hours). Come hungry and order a good beer to wash it down (my recommendation is the "Torres del Paine" from Austral).

Address: Carretera Austral, next to the previously mentioned restaurants

+ **Breakfast Restaurant Tamara (breakfast for 8 USD)**

The only place in town where you can grab breakfast. Nevertheless, it is still pretty basic: you get scrambled eggs, bread, butter, and marmalade with tea/(instant) coffee.

Address: across the street from the gas station.

Accommodation in Puerto Rio Tranquilo

Another town in which you most likely need to get you accommodation sorted right after arrival (try to arrive a bit earlier).

Both times I stayed in the very basic hospedaje "Sylvana" in a double room with bathroom ensuite was about 27 USD (no breakfast, no Wi-Fi).
E-Mail: silvanapinuer@gmail.com, Cell: +56 9 94138195

The biggest and best-looking option was the Hosteria Costanera. It is also the only one I found that you can reserve in advance.
E-Mail: ipinuerhostal@gmail.com, Cell: +56 9 5743 2175

Update (March'2017): The town got very popular lately, so try to book your accommodation in advance (best bet is to call the mentioned)!

Get Out

Chile Chico   - ca. 4,5hrs
(Buses Becker)

Cochrane   - ca. 4hrs
(Buses Becker)

Coyhaique   - ca. 5,5hrs
(Buses Becker, Acuario, Sao Paulo)

Notes:

Cochrane & Tortel

The biggest city in the southern part of the Carretera Austral is Cochrane. Between Cochrane and Lago General Carrera, the road passes through a picturesque river landscape where the turquoise Rio Baker winds through the valley.

Further down south, you should consider going to Caleta Tortel, a village that was partially built on timber piles.

Get In

The further south you drive on the Carrtera Austral, the longer and harder it gets.

Coming from the north: Cochrane is located about a 3.5-hour drive from Puerto Rio Tranquilo and a five-hour drive from Chile Chico. As mentioned in the introduction, the stretch along the Rio Baker is picturesque. Consider a layover there (there are campgrounds and some guesthouses).

Coming from the south, it is a four-hour drive from Tortel and a very long nine-hour drive from Villa O'Higgins involving a ferry crossing (check the schedule before departure!). For the drive from Villa O'Higgins to Tortel you should plan about 7.5 hours.

Things to See & Do

You should bring some time if you plan on doing the following activities as it will always involve a lot of driving because of the distances and remoteness of the area. If you plan on going down to Villa O'Higgins afterward (or if you care to come from there), you should stop by in Caleta Tortel.

✦ Rio Baker

The Rio Baker is considered the river with the biggest rapids in the country and is, therefore, also a very good place for rafting.

This is why you'll find some tour operators on the way to Cochrane, e.g. in Puerto Bertrand.

✦ Parque Patagonia

Another insider tip is one of the newest National Parks of Patagonia and the latest project of the recently deceased Douglas Thompkins: the Parque Patagonia. The area is situated northeast of Cochrane and has several great day hikes and multi-day treks to offer.

Route suggestions and maps can be found on the park's website (see link list).

✦ Caleta Tortel

The only place I haven't visited so far, but absolutely belongs on this list is Tortel. After talking with locals, as well as seeing pictures and hearing reviews from fellow travelers, I realized that this timber-pile-founded village is worth a visit. However, it is almost impossible to get to Caleta Tortel by hitchhiking (which I did both times). However, now there is a regular minibus service from Cochrane.

Restaurants

✦ **Rayito de Sol (main for 7.5 USD)**

Right next to Taxi Katalina (here, you can get tickets for the bus ride to Tortel and Villa O'Higgins) you can find this tiny restaurant. The selection is limited but everything is homemade and budget friendly.

Accommodation in Cochrane

And again—you guessed it—it is all about the hrs method. You can find some hosterias and rooms in the center of the town.

I can particularly recommend "Hostal Central" (Calle Teniente Merino 347, Cochrane). A double room with ensuite bathroom ended up costing 42 USD. The Wi-Fi was comparably good but there was no breakfast.

They also offer Cabanas, single and budget-friendly dorms.

Get Out

Tortel   - ca. 4hrs
(bus service provided by Taxi Katalina)

Villa O'Higgins   - ca. 9hrs
(bus service provided by Taxi Katalina)

Pto. Rio Tranquilo - ca. 4hrs
(Buses Becker)

Villa O'Higgins

The end of the Carretera Austral has a special vibe and is surrounded by glaciers, mountains, and plenty of water. It's a paradise for hikers and mountaineers.

Again, a longer stay here to take on the unknown walks and expeditions in the area around Villa O'Higgins is worth the effort.

Get In

Villa O'Higgins is without a doubt the most remote but, at the same time, most beautiful village on the Carretera Austral. To get here, it takes you at least a full day of traveling.

The fastest option is coming from the north. From Tortel, the drive is about 7.5 hours; from Cochrane, it's about nine hours (both options involve a ferry crossing—check the schedule!)

You can also get in from El Chaltén in Argentina: a combination of minibus, hiking, and a boat makes it possible. This little adventure takes normally two days and requires an overnight stay at the farm Candelario Mansilla at Lake O'Higgins' shore. You can find a detailed description about this in the trekking guide!

Things to See & Do

✦ Mirador

Right in the center, you can hike up (10mins) to a newly constructed viewpoint (just around the corner of the Plaza de Armas)—a good sunset option!

✦ O'Higgins Glacier & Lake

As you can see, there are countless glaciers along the Carretera Austral but this one is particularly impressive as it carves into the turquoise Lago O'Higgins and is difficult to get to.

From Villa O'Higgins, a boat goes to the glacier approximately every 2-3 days in the summer.

When you make your way down to Villa O'Higgins it would be a shame to miss out on the glacier—though it isn't that cheap, it is definitely worth it.

The roundtrip to the glacier is a day trip and will end up costing about 150 USD, but if you only go one way (e.g. you want to cross into El Chaltén) the additional price to see the glacier is only 75 USD.

Find more information about the schedule and prices over at Robinson Crusoe (see link list).

Backpacking in Chile

✦ Two Day Trip to El Chaltén

In addition, the same boat allows the trek to El Chaltén, starting from the Candelario Mansilla farm. All in all, it's a 2-3 day undertaking from Villa O'Higgins, but it is definitely worthwhile. I've done this tour twice, once from El Chalten and once from Villa O'Higgins. It is also possible to start the tour to the glacier from Candelario Mansilla, as the boat stops here first to leave disembarking passengers who only booked the crossing before it goes to the glacier and then again around Candelario Mansilla back to Villa O'Higgins.

I wrote a detailed description of the whole journey and how to do it; you can find it in the Trekking Guide section of this guide!

✦ Day hike to the Alta Vista Viewpoint (18 km)

This smooth day hike leads you to altogether three viewpoints and is located just outside of town.

At the highest point, you can see Laguna Negra and the peaks of the Southern Patagonian ice field (see the photo at the beginning).

Find a description of this trail in the trekking guide.

✦ Day Hike to the Mosco glacier (21 km)

Unfortunately, I haven't done this hike myself (yet!) but it is known to be one of the best hiking experiences in the area and is well marked. The path leads along the Mosco River up to the glacier the river is fed by. It is recommended you have some hiking experience.

The GPS coordinates & a description for the hike can be found on a website (see link list).

Restaurants

✦ Green, peaked house, near Plaza de Armas (daily dish for 8-10 USD)

Unfortunately, this restaurant didn't have a sign as it just opened at the time I was there in 2016. It is located on a street off the Plaza de Armas (when you stand in front of the library and then head to the left, you'll see a very uniquely shaped house on the left side. There are also some colorful garbage bins in front of the house).

I ate here twice, as the food offered was homemade and prepared by the owner. There is only a tiny selection, depending on what they have in stock (remember how remote this place is). I had Pichanga once and a steak a lá Pobre the next day. Altogether, a very good deal for this area!

✦ Empanadas (1 USD each)

If you prefer a more budget-friendly option, you can find an empanaderia in the same street (a little bit further, right-hand side)—homemade empanadas fresh out of the oven. Tasty!

Accommodation in Villa O'Higgins

I stayed both times in the legendary El Mosco Hostel. This cozy, modern hostel is one of the biggest accommodation options in the area and the place to be for all sorts of travelers.

On my first trip, I stayed in a dorm (self-catering or you pay extra for a breakfast provided by the hostel). However, last time I stayed in one of their comfy double rooms on the first floor with ensuite bathroom and a rich breakfast included (eggs, sandwich, homemade bread, marmalade, butter, honey, cake, juice, coffee or tea).

They also offer camping and a cabana (a perfect option if you come with a group).

The open kitchen is the meeting point. If it is warm outside, the terrace with several hammocks is the place to be. The hostel also provides free Wi-Fi and good tips from Filli who is the "hostel mother".

You should make a reservation in advance via email. Consider that it takes some time until you get an answer as the Wi-Fi is very slow in Villa O'Higgins.

Find all the info needed, as well as prices, and contact on the website.

If you like to treat yourself you should consider staying at the Robinson Crusoe Lodge! A very stylish mix of luxury and log cabin flair…and they also have a hot tub :)

Apart from this, the Lodge offers a diverse tour program including boat trips on the O'Higgins lake (this company owns the boat which takes you to the glacier).

You can find the link to book these hostels/hotels inside the link list I provided.

Get Out

Tortel   - ca. 7,5hrs
(bus service provided by Taxi Katalina)

Cochrane   - ca. 9hrs
(bus service provided by Taxi Katalina)

El Chaltén, Argentina   - 2 days
(see Trekking guide)

Notes:

Puerto Natales

Puerto Natales is the hot spot for lovers of the outdoors as it is the starting point for adventures at the Torres del Paine National Park. The small town is home to many stores and shops to help you to prepare for your hiking trip.

Get In

The quickest is connections by plane as the airport of Punta Arenas is quite close. Another airport to fly to is El Calafate in Argentina (beware of visa costs that might apply in Argentina for your nationality!). From both cities, you have regular bus connections to Puerto Natales.

Apart from bus and air transport, you can also go by ferry from Puerto Montt—the company that offers this route is called Navimag.

Things to See & Do

✦ Torres del Paine

Without a doubt, the highlight in this part of Patagonia and the #1 reason to come to Puerto Natales!

On a multi-day trek, you see much diversity in a short amount of time: glaciers, forests, impressive mountain ranges, lagoons, and picturesque valleys. However, ensure you reserve the camps long in advance!

Find all information needed in the trekking guide for Torres del Paine!

Restaurants / Cafés / Bars

✦ Mesita Grande (Restaurant) - 10 USD / Meal

If you want to treat yourself with a proper meal after finishing your trek, this is the right place to visit. Here, you get tasty pizza served on a long table where you mingle with fellow hikers and are can exchange your hiking stories.

Highly recommended!

✦ Baguales (Brewery & Bar) - 3 USD/Beer

Best bar in town - try the home brew!

✦ El Living (Restaurant/Café, Vegetarian Options) - 6-9 USD / Meal

This is probably the coziest restaurant and café you'll find in town. On the board, you'll find the daily dish. There is also a good selection of homemade vegetarian options.

Besides the soups, I can highly recommend the sweet treats! The place is a family-run business and the owners are lovely.

Unterkunft in Puerto Natales

The eco hostel named Yagan House was my home for almost two weeks and is the perfect starting point for your hiking adventures. I liked the relaxed atmosphere and the cozy common areas, it somehow felt more like a mountain lodge than a usual hostel.

The owner, Paulina, and her staff are sympathetic and helpful: you can book bus tickets and organize other activities like kayaking or trips to El Calafate.

In addition, the breakfast was great: homemade bread, yogurt, cereals, butter, marmalade, freshly made scrambled eggs, tea, and coffee are a good base for your first day of hiking in the park. On top of that, you have a lot of extra services like a luggage room, laundry, rental of hiking equipment, and a small house bar (beer, wine, pisco sour, hot chocolate, brownies).

Positive: there are four bathrooms so you never have to wait, great service, cozy atmosphere, luggage room for your time on the trek, nice staff

Downsides: the Internet is sometimes very unstable (we had to restart the router quite often)

Prices: Dorm (4 Bed) from 22 USD, Private from 30 USD

Address: O'Higgins 584

I can offer you a great giveaway! If you use the discount code "holagringo yagan house" when checking in, you get a free laundry per booking. This is a great chance to start on the trek with fresh clothes or to get them clean afterward while chilling in the cozy living room.

Fully booked?

No worries, there are plenty other great options in Puerto Natales. You can find the link to book the Yagan House and an overview of options, as well as ratings by other guests, in Puerto Natales inside the link list I provided.

Get Out

Punta Arenas	- 3 hrs (Buses Fernandez)
El Calafate (Arg)	- 7 hrs (Buses Pacheco)
Ushuaia (Arg)	- 15 hrs
Torres del Paine	- 2-3 hrs (Buses Pacheco and many others)

Punta Arenas

The largest city in southern Chile was once a central trading hub in the Americas until the Panama channel was completed. Nowadays, an increasing number of tourists visit Punta Arenas and use it as a transportation hub for Torres del Paine and to visit the nearby penguin colony.

Get In

If you're coming from Santiago, taking a flight is the best option as the long distance bus connection is too long and complicated.

From Argentina, you have regular bus connections: from Ushuaia (Tolka Turismo, 12 hrs) as well as from El Calafate (Bus Sur, 10 hrs).

Things to See & Do

✦ Isla Magdalena (approx. 35 USD)

Try to squeeze Isla Magdalena into your schedule as it is close to Punta Arenas.

This small island is home to 50,000 penguins that you can visit for 30mins with a boat leaving from Punta Arenas. Avoid visiting at the end of the season, as the penguins migrate to the north for the winter!

✦ Promenade & Inner City

Along the Strait of Magellan, you'll find a long promenade that is perfect for a run or a walk.

The inner city isn't as impressive but there are some nice houses around the central square.

Restaurants / Cafés / Bars

✦ La Marmita (Restaurant) --- 10-15 USD / Meal

On my last trip, I ate here twice, which says a lot about the quality of the food. Besides the tasty regional dishes, I enjoyed the atmosphere and interior. Reservation recommended for high season!

✦ Mesita Grande (Restaurant) --- 9-12 USD / Mahlzeit

The restaurant in Puerto Natales is so popular they decided to open a second one in Punta Arenas. As tasty and popular as the original!

Accommodation in Punta Arenas

La Estancia Hostel & Hotel is a calm, well-equipped accommodation that feels more like a hotel.

La Estancia has several private rooms and is perfectly located with only a few hundred meters from the bus terminal and offers a lovely breakfast.

Fully booked?

No worries, there are plenty other great options in Punta Arenas. You can find the link of options in Punta Arenas, as well as ratings by other guests, inside the link list I provided.

Get Out

If you arrived from the North I recommend continuing to Ushuaia!

Puerto Natales   - 3 hrs
(Buses Fernandez)

El Calafate (Arg)   - 10 hrs
(Bus Sur)

Ushuaia (Arg)   - 12 hrs
(Company: Tolka Turismo / Bus-Sur / Pacheco)

Notes:

My personal Chile Insider Tips

Chile offers great infrastructure for tourists and has invested a lot of money to promote their attractions all over the world. Nevertheless, there are still some places that are relatively off the beaten path.

Here are some of those spots:

- **Termas de Chillan** (in winter season), close to Concepcion, is a great little ski resort. The best place to stay is called "Mi-Lodge".

- **El Cani in Pucón** – this private park isn't covered in many guide books. You need a private guide to see the impressive nature inside the former crater of a volcano.

- **Hanging Glacier of Queulat** and hot springs close to Puyuhuapi.

- Rafting at the **Futaleufú River.**

- **Laguna San Rafael NP** near Puerto Rio Tranquilo.

- **Caleta Tortel** located in the very south of the Carretera Austral (last village before Villa O'Higgins)—most of the village is timber-pile founded. Very scenic!

- **O'Higgins Glacier** – in Villa O'Higgins, you can go on a boat excursion to one of the most remote glaciers in that region!

- The **Q/O in Torres del Paine** – The W is the most popular trek in Torres del Paine but you won't see the massive South Patagonian ice field and the picturesque Refugio Dickson that way. Go for the longer hike, as it is all worth it (and less crowded)

Notes:

4 TREKKING GUIDE CARRETERA AUSTRAL

The lesser known part of Patagonia has some great hikes to offer. Here, you can find a tiny section of treks I did myself and can highly recommend.

Of course, there are many more hikes. For these, you should check the website of the Parque Patagonia (great source!) and the website for the hikes around Chaitén (see link list) as well as the recommended guides at the end of this book.

1) Day hike to Cerro Castillo, Villa Cerro Castillo

(ca. 20 km, 1 day, medium difficulty)

Beside the four-day version from Horquetas Grandes, you can take on a day hike to see the Cerro Castillo with its glacier and the incredibly colored lagoon. However, you should be prepared for the steep ascent and start your day early with a good breakfast and calculate 8-9 hours depending on your fitness level.

The starting point of the hike is located outside of town. From Coyhaique you'd need to turn right at the first intersection (you get to the center if you turn left). The gravel road you're on then leads you down to a bridge that you need to cross (fill up your water reserves at that stream!). After that, you get to a tiny ranger hut where you need to pay a fee of 5000 CLP (= 8 USD) per person. The ranger will also give you some useful information about the hike and the route.

First, you need to go through two gates before taking on the first tiny ascent. Afterward, you must walk through an open area until you reach the forest. After more gates (remember to close them every time you cross) the trail goes upwards until you reach an area full of bushes. Follow the narrow paths that lead upward.

After about two hours of hiking, the terrain changes again. It gets rockier and the trail winds are stronger. The view over the Ibanez valley from here is breathtaking. Use the chance to take a break and enjoy the views. Around lunchtime, you should arrive at the viewpoint. Use the tiny stupas and red metal poles as guidance. You should get to a point where you see the Cerro Castillo and the blue lagoon in all its glory. If you still have enough energy and time left, you can go down to the lagoon and have your lunch break there.

To get back to town you simply use the same trail you used coming up here. Start early to get back before the sunset!

2) Day Hike to Mirador Altavista, Villa O'Higgins

(16 km, 1 day, easy)

The surroundings of Villa O'Higgins are a paradise for outdoor lovers. This day hike is a popular route that offers a great view and is altogether relatively easy. Before you go, I recommend charging up your smartphone and having the "Maps.Me" app with the offline map of Chile ready (ideally, you downloaded the whole map before the trip with decent Wi-Fi) as the trail is sometimes hard to find but the viewpoints and the trail are marked on that particular map. Don't forget to take some snacks and water.

Start your hike in the morning and head in the direction of the harbor/end of the Carretera Austral. After about 2km, the road leads over a big metal bridge. The trail starts right after that bridge on the right (there is a big sign). We found it fenced and decided to climb over the fence to follow the path.

The path leads upwards through the forest. After about an hour, you get to the first viewpoint. Afterward, the trail takes you to a thin forest to the next viewpoint; ensure that you check your position with the Maps.Me app every now and then as the marks are partially missing or overgrown.

We often lost the trail and used the GPS to find it after only a few hundred meters later. Around lunchtime (depending on when you started), you should get to the viewpoint Mirador Altavista where you can enjoy a phenomenal view of Villa O'Higgins and the Mosco Valley with its glaciers. If you follow the trail further, you can also see the Laguna Negra and the white peaks of the Southern Patagonian ice field.

To get back to Villa O'Higgins, you use the same trail.

Steve Hänisch

3) Border Crossing Villa O'Higgins - El Chaltén

(57 km, 2 days, medium difficulty)

If you plan on exploring Southern Patagonia after your Carretera Austral adventure, this is the best option to get from the end of Ruta 7 to Argentina. I did this challenging crossing twice. The first time (2013), I came from Argentina heading to Villa O'Higgins; the second time (2016), I did it vice versa (as described here).

Be aware that this is anything but a normal border crossing as there are no continuous roads in this area let alone public transport to get you from Villa O'Higgins to El Chaltén. The reason for that is the border conflict both countries have been involved in and still partially are. Today, the actual border is situated a bit north of the Lago del Desert in no man's land but the border posts of both countries lie 21 km apart.

Nevertheless, this crossing is doable with a combination of minibuses, boats, and a hike within two days. For this, you should be capable carrying all your luggage on a 21km hike with you (needless to say, suitcases aren't a good idea). In high season, it is sometimes possible to book transport of the luggage for the whole trekking part with a combination of cars and horses. I intended to do that last time but it was only possible for part of the trail (I needed to carry all the stuff for a good 6km or so. That was last time I went with some heavy camera gear). This is why you shouldn't plan for this option, as there are several factors that could leave you stranded with the luggage (weather or the owner isn't there etc.)—though I feel like you get priority treatment when booking all of this with Robinson Crusoe in advance (at least three days before!).

If you want to organize the luggage transport yourself, you should contact Ricardo in advance. He is the owner of the farm Candelario Mancilla and operates the transport depending on his mood and the number of requests. In order to do so, you must speak Spanish and expect long reply times: ricardolevican@hotmail.com (yes, he is also a very special character).

As stated, the crossing is possible in both directions but you should take a look at the boat schedule of Robinson Crusoe, which handles the transfer between Villa O'Higgins and Candelario Mancilla as it only operates on certain dates.

You'll most likely spend the night at the small farm Candelario Mancilla or at their campground (very basic but nicely located). The company that operates the boat is named "Robinson Crusoe" and offers also a transfer between Villa O'Higgins and the dock by bus as well as vouchers for the boat on the Lago del Desierto and the van that takes you from Lago del Desert to El Chaltén. This sums up to a proper amount of money but let me tell you that this border crossing is a unique experience! Often, you can pay for the whole experience even by credit card (if their Wi-Fi works) which is a rare occasion on the Carretera Austral.

Furthermore, you can use the chance to book the additional tour to the O'Higgins glacier, an experience only a few hundred visitors get to do per year. This addition to the crossing involves an additional five hours of time and extra costs. The tour is usually executed after the boat arrived at Candelario Mancilla (here, passengers who only booked the crossing leave the boat, passengers who book the tour from Candelario Mancilla get on). After the glacier, the boat first stops at Candelario Mancilla again (passengers like you get off/ other passengers who only booked the crossing to Villa O'Higgins get on) before it returns to Villa O'Higgins in the afternoon. In comparison to glacier tours in the popular tourist destinations of Patagonia, this one is relatively cheap so I recommend considering it!

As the boat leaves Villa O'Higgins pretty early in the morning, you get to Candelario Mancilla before lunchtime if you don't want to do the glacier tour. If you feel like it, you can do the hike on this day and use the chance to camp out at the free campsite on the northern lakeshore (you'd need camping equipment). In case you are a very fit and fast hiker (21km with luggage) or you have the whole transfer to the Lago del Desierto organized (you need to hike the last 6km). You can even get to the boat on the Lago del Desierto on time and make the whole crossing in just one day.

Regarding communication, I highly recommend a good knowledge of Spanish. From El Chaltén, you can use my Argentina guide where I list the must-dos, restaurants, and hikes on that side of Patagonia (besides all the other destinations in Argentina).

Please consider taking enough cash with you before embarking on this adventure as you'll only find 2 ATMs in El Chaltén which can run out of money in high season. So I recommend bringing Chilean Peso or even better: USD. In comparison to 2013, I was also able to pay more often with my credit card (ask at the reception if they accept cards before checking in to accommodation).

I produced a short documentary about my border crossing experience including the glacier tour and the hikes in El Chaltén - watch it to get an idea what it is like (see link list)!

Backpacking in Chile

1) Villa O'Higgins - Candelario Mansilla (Day 1)

The minibus takes you from the Robinson Crusoe Lodge (right across the street from the Mosco Hostel) to the dock early in the morning where the boat is waiting for you (the transfer has an additional fee of 4 USD and needs to be booked in advance when buying the boat tickets!). The bus ride takes about 15 minutes.

Before embarking, you should use the chance to take a photo with the sign that states the end of the Carretera Austral. The sign can be found right next to the dock.

The boat takes you across the O'Higgins Lake first to Candelario Mancilla (70 USD). Depending on the weather, you'll get there after 2.5 hours at about 11/11:30 a.m. In case you booked the glacier tour (50 USD), you can stay on the boat. Otherwise, you need to leave the boat here and you can start your hike to the Lago del Desierto (continue with (2) of this itinerary) or stay at Candelario Mancilla.

If you do the glacier excursion, you'll get back to Candelario Mancilla by 5/5:30 p.m. and leave the boat.

From the dock, follow the path and turn left at the first junction to the farm Candelario Mancilla. Here, you can stay in a room (about 12 USD) or on the campground (3 USD). For both, you need to check in at the farm with the owners. You also have the option of having dinner (9 USD) and/or breakfast (4 USD) at the farm. I recommend going for the dinner.

Consider: Right now there is at least one other operator who offers the transfer across O'Higgins Lake to the farm but there is no certain schedule or any option to book it in advance as it is a local guy who does it occasionally. You can only ask in the village (Villa O'Higgins) to get more information. Both times, I used the service by Robinson Crusoe where everything worked out as planned. That is why I recommend using them, as they are more reliable and have been doing this for years.

2) Candelario Mancilla - Lago del Desierto (Day 2)

You should start as early as possible (8 a.m.) if you want to catch the boat at the Lago del Desierto. The 21km hike takes a lot of time when you have to carry all your luggage as you'd need more breaks.

After a few minutes, you'll get to the Chilean border post where you need to get your passport stamped. Then, for the first 15km, you'll follow a gravel road that goes upwards until you reach the forest. Here, the trail flattens out and you get to see the Fitz Roy in the distance for the first time if the weather is good.

You'll get to an airfield after a while. From here, it is only a few kilometers until you get to the actual border, which is marked by a construction made of steel and two big signs stating you're leaving Chile and entering Argentina.

The last 6km the gravel road turns into a narrow hiking trail that leads you through the forest over little streams and a muddy swamp (if you didn't get your feet wet until here, you certainly will now). Shortly after the trail winds its way steeply downhill (great view to the Lago del Desert and the Fitz Roy) to the northern shore of the Lago del Desierto, you'll find the Argentinian border post and a free campground.

Make sure to go to the passport control to officially enter Argentina. Afterward, you have two options. You can take the boat to cross the lake (30 USD, only during high season) or you can camp at the free campsite and start hiking to the southern shore of the lake the next morning (5 hours, 12 km).

The crossing with the boat takes about 30 minutes.

3) Lago del Desierto - El Chaltén

To cover the last 37 km to El Chaltén, you should organize a transfer in advance that is synced with the times of the boat on the Lago del Desierto. In Villa O'Higgins, you can do so when booking at the Robinson Crusoe office.

The minibus/van will be waiting for you at the parking not far from the dock on the southern shore. The ride to El Chaltén takes about 1.5 hours.

Another option is to hitchhike to El Chaltén. During high season, you can find some day tourists coming visiting the lake and the nearby Huemul glacier. Sometimes, tour operators have free spots left and take you for a fee to El Chaltén.

In my guide for Argentina, you'll find a lot of information about El Chaltén and the hikes you should do there. If you are an experienced hiker, I highly recommend the Huemul circuit nearby El Chaltén, which is one of my favorite treks in Patagonia!

Notes:

5 TREKKING GUIDE TORRES DEL PAINE

Personally, the national park Torres del Paine is my number one attraction in Patagonia. You should take some time and do a multi-day trek to experience as much of it as possible: glaciers, forests, impressive mountain ranges, lagoons, and rivers.

Here, you'll find all the info needed on how to prepare for hiking in Torres del Paine. Even the Lonely Planet considers the trails here as some of the world's best trekking routes.

I hiked the "Q" in 2013 and did the circuit again in 2016; altogether, I spent three weeks in the park. During my times there, I hiked the W, the circuit, and the Q on my own. Furthermore, I spent a lot of time with the locals, as well as guides and park rangers, who helped me to gather information to provide a broad guide.

Preparation

The standard starting point for the park is usually the small town of Puerto Natales. Situated 112 km south of the national park, it offers regular buses that will pick you up directly at your hostel and drive you to the park.

The nearest airport is located in Punta Arenas (3 hrs by bus). Another option is the airport in El Calafate (Argentina) but here you need to consider possible visa fees as well as a longer bus ride of about five hours to get to Puerto Natales.

1) Bus to Torres del Paine / Transportation Inside

Get In

Nearly every hostel in Puerto Natales sells return tickets but prices can vary between 15.000 (= 20 € / 22 USD, directly at the office of the bus company inside the bus terminal) and 18.000 CLP (at the hostel). By buying a return ticket, you can leave the date of return open so you can extend or shorten your stay in the park as you wish. Buses leave Puerto Natales at 7:30 a.m. and 2:30 p.m. and will need 2.5 hours to arrive at the park entrance (Laguna Amarga).

Beside the entrance, there are two more stops afterward in the park: Pudeto an hour later, where you can catch the boat to Paine Grande (see below), and the Administration, which is about 2 hours later.

Bus companies who offer daily services are Buses Gomez, Buses Fernandez, Buses Maria José, and Bus Sur (offers also a connection from Punta Arenas).

Transport inside the Park

Inside the park, you can take a boat that connects Pudeto and the campsite/refugio Paine Grande. The catamaran will cost you 15.000 CLP one way (= 20 € / 22 USD) and 23.000 CLP (= 30 € / 33 USD) for an open return ticket.

During high season, the boat leaves from Pudeto at 09:30 a.m., 12:00 p.m. and 6:00 p.m. and will take around 30 minutes. The other way, it leaves at 10:00 a.m., 12:30 p.m. (bus connection), and 6:30 p.m. (bus connection).

For more information and updated schedules, also check certain catamaran info page on the official Torres del Paine website (see link list).

Another option inside the park is to take a mini shuttle

between the entrance and the Hotel Las Torres. After arriving at the park, just go there, hop on, and pay 2.800 CLP (= 4 € / 5 USD). It takes just a few minutes. For the way back, it leaves around 30-45 mins before the bus to Puerto Natales arrives at the entrance.

The 3rd option is a rather expensive one where you'll need additional transport inside the park to get to the Lago Grey Pier. From here, you can take a boat to Refugio Grey for about 50000 CLP (= 64 € / 72 USD) one way. The same is possible vice versa. For both options, you should book in advance. The whole service is offered by the Hotel Lago Grey, so it makes sense to stay there if you want to do this.

Get Out

There are two scheduled departures at the same bus stops. The early bus leaves from the Administration at 1 p.m., from Pudeto at 1:30 p.m., and from the entrance at 2:30 p.m.

The late bus leaves from the Administration at 6 p.m., from Pudeto at 7 p.m., and from the entrance (Laguna Amarga) at 7:45 p.m.

2) Camping in Torres del Paine & Refugios

I recommend using your own tent/renting a tent in Puerto Natales and camping at the campsites. Nevertheless, it is technically possible to hike at least the W without camping by sleeping in the Refugios...however, this is expensive and almost impossible to do in high season (you need to book too far in advance!)

Make sure to book all your campsites/refugios in advance as the number of visitors has increased dramatically in recent years!

Consider: cooking is only allowed at campsites/refugios. Open fires are not allowed anywhere in the park. The same goes for camping in general.

Refugios & Domes

A bed will be around 35-60 USD in a dorm and you have to pay extra for breakfast (around 14 USD) and sheets or bring a sleeping bag.

The main refugios offer a range of services besides accommodation, such as tent rental, meals (both to be booked in advance!), kiosks, electricity, some even have a bar and (expensive, slow) Wi-Fi.

The refugios are operated by two different companies and it is recommended that you book everything in advance, especially in the high season:

- Refugios/Dome Tents operated by fantastico sur:
  Los Cuernos, El Chileno, Torres (next to Hotel Las Torres), El Frances, Seron.

- Refugios operated by Vertice Patagonia:
  Dickson, Paine Grande, Grey

Free Campsites

Wohoo – free accommodation! Yeah, that sounds good, huh? Unfortunately, there are just a few and some of them might be closed. So, if you want to do one of the big treks, you have to stay at paid campsites in between. The setup for a free camp is always the same: you have a rain-covered construction to cook in, places to set up your tent, toilets, and water (mostly from a stream).

Please head to the official reservation system to reserve your spot at the free CONAF campsites in advance (see link list). Please consider that you can stay for one night only.

Reservations are mandatory. If a campsite is fully booked, you need to adjust your itinerary.

The free campsites are:

- Campamento Torres (reservation mandatory!)
- Campamento Paso (reservation recommended)
- Campamento Las Carretas
- Campamento Italiano (reservation mandatory!)

You'll find also Britanico and Japones, but they are for climbers with a certain license only.

Consider: You always have to take your garbage with you and you should wash dishes away from the stream. I highly encourage that you take this seriously and remind fellow campers who don't respect the rules to protect the environment!

Paid Campsites

There are two kinds of paid campsites: private campsites and the ones next to a refugio. The prices vary. Usually, the ones next to a refugio are more expensive.

The difference between both is the facilities they offer. Private campsites offer a place to cook, toilets, showers, and water, as well as a small shop. At the refugios, you have the possibility of using the restaurant, a mini market, and sometimes you have plugs to charge your camera batteries.

At the refugios, you have the possibility of using the restaurant, a mini market, and sometimes you have electric outlets to charge the batteries of your camera. Moreover, you'll have the chance to rent tents, sleeping bags, and even mats.

The paid campsites are also operated by fantastico sur and Vertice Patagonia. Reservations are a MUST during high season (to be done through their websites).

Here are all the campsites with prices (per night, per person):

- Refugio Paine Grande, Vertice
  (7000 CLP = 10 USD)

- Campamento Francés, fantastico sur
  (8500/9500 CLP = 14 USD) [This one is new and is not marked on my trail map; it is located between Los Cuernos and Italiano]

- Refugio Los Cuernos, fantastico sur
  (7500/8500 CLP = 12 USD)

- Refugio Chileno, fantastico sur
  (only with reservation 7500/8500 = 12 USD)

- Campamento Serón, fantastico sur
  (8500/9500 CLP = 14 USD)

- Refugio Dickson, Vertice (6000 CLP = 9 USD)

- Campamento Los Perros, CONAF/Vertice
  (6000 CLP = 9 USD)

- Refugio Grey, Vertice
  (6000 CLP = 9 USD)

- Campamento Torres/Central, fantastico sur
  [next to Hotel Las Torres] (8500/9500 CLP = 14 USD)

Hotel inside the national park & tours

Do you want to add a bit of luxury to the end of your hike? Then this is a great option to not only spend more time inside the park but also to explore more and eat some great food!

I got the chance to spend four days at Hotel Las Torres Patagonia in 2016 after I finished the circuit trek and used it to explore the spots you don't get to see when hiking. The fact that the area in which the hotel is located is a private area owned by the hotel makes it possible to explore this part of the park on horses. My personal highlight was the rather tough horse riding/hiking combination up to the Cerro Paine, which is opposite to the Torres and offers a unique view, a tour offered exclusively by the hotel (only three groups went up there in 2016!).

The hotel itself is, hands down, definitely an upscale choice but offers the best location inside the park (perfect base for photographers), great tours, and is a good choice for those who want to explore the park with day trips. Though a bit pricey, the rooms are comfortable, the food and the bar are very good. Wi-Fi is also included (but not as fast because of the location).

For those who finish the trip here but won't stay at the hotel, you are welcome to have a bite or a drink at the bar, which has a lovely view of the Paine Massif before you leave to catch your transfer back to Puerto Natales.

3) Weather Conditions & Clothes to Take

First of all, in Patagonia, you can have basically everything in one day. This means, snow, rain, and sun. You'll always have very strong winds to deal with. This means up to more than 100 km/h.

In summer, you should be prepared to temperatures until below 0°C. In winter, it can be quite cold.

I personally recommend hiking during the shoulder season October/November and March/April to avoid the crowds (depending on the exact date you might also not need to book camp sites in advance).

The high season in Torres del Paine lasts from the 1st of October to the 30th of April and the low season from the 1st of May to the 30th of September. Though the park is open all year round, most trails, camp sites, and refugios are closed in winter (May-August).

If you still want to hike in winter, you need to get in touch with CONAF. Come well prepared and consider going with a guide as trails are hard to find after snowfall (there is no maintenance during that time of year).

It's always best to check the weather before you go, even though the forecast is not reliable and weather can change quite quickly. Therefore, it is better to be prepared for everything. Even in summer, I recommend taking a jumper for the colder parts of the trek like the John Gardner Pass. In winter, you should add layers of warm clothes.

Speaking of clothes, you'll find everything in the Patagonia Packing List, which you can find later in this guide!

Consider: In February, I used to trek with a thermal shirt and long pants all the time. When it rained, I kept walking (believe me, you will not melt and will not get sick as long as you are moving. Only use the rain jacket when you are in the camp or make a stop).

Furthermore, I had two of each. This means walking clothes and dry clothes for the camps. I never mixed it, so I always had a set of dry clothes in my bag.

4) Which food to take for hiking in Torres del Paine?

When I have been on the trek, I saw a different kind of strategy—basically, deciding what to take depends on the individual for a multi-day hike. As I planned, for nine full days my main focus was to pack as lightly as possible because food will be the heaviest part in your backpack in that case.

Therefore, I stuck to (all packed into Zip-Lock bags):

– porridge and dry fruits for breakfast + tea/coffee

– salami, cereal bars, snickers, dry fruits and nuts for lunch (small snacks to eat while short breaks)

– 200g rice or 200g pasta for dinner
+ sauce (sauce powder or soup powder)
+ cheese/salami to add more flavor ;)

Moreover, it's always nice to have some chocolate and sweeties to treat yourself. In addition, a small amount of alcohol is not a bad idea for cold nights (I took 200ml of pisco – also cool to celebrate the finish of a steep trail).

The second great option I got to try on my recent hiking trip in 2016 was to take lightweight freeze dried meals. Those meals are easy to prepare; they don't take much space and they don't taste too bad. If you want to go for this option, you should definitely buy them at home or online and take them to Chile with you. Please make sure the meals meet the customs' regulations in Chile as they are strict about organic products. You might need to declare it on arrival.

Tip:
I drank water from the streams. You'll have a stream nearly every 20 minutes when hiking. I simply used my cup to drink the water, which has the best quality one can find.

At the campsites and the busier parts of the park, you should be careful. Go a bit up the stream and consider purifying using a SteriPen (see link list) to ensure you drink clean water (there are some stupid people washing their dishes in the water, which is strictly forbidden and led to problems with water quality in 2016 where several hikers got sick!).

So, just take a small bottle with you for the time in between and purify water when needed.

5) Costs to Calculate (Entrance & Shops)

As mentioned, the Torres del Paine is stunning and is, therefore, very popular.

Apart from the costs already mentioned for campsites and transportation, you should calculate the following as well:

- the entrance fee is 18,000 CLP (= 26 USD) in high season and 10.000 CLP in low season for foreigners (children pay 500, Chileans pay 3.000 CLP)
- sweeties (M&Ms, chocolate bars) at mini-shops in refugios are between 1,000 – 2,000 CLPs
- soft drinks at mini-shops are between 1,500 and 2,500 CLPs
- beer is between 2,000 and 3,000 CLPs

Notes:

Patagonia Packing List for Trekking & Camping

This Patagonia packing list will help you to prepare for your outdoor adventure in one of the most stunning regions of South America.

I created this list based on my Patagonia trekking experiences in Chile as well as Argentina in the following regions: Torres del Paine, Los Glaciares, Carretera Austral, Esquel, and Bariloche.

1) Backpack & Bags

Let's start with the essentials – a good trekking backpack is needed to carry all your stuff around. For this, you should get one that is comfortable, adjustable, spacious, and durable.

- [ ] Trekking backpack – e.g. the Osprey Atmos 50 is great for multiple day hikes, for big tours the Osprey Aether 70 or Deuter AirContact are good choices
- [ ] If you plan only short hikes: Hiking Daypack
- [ ] Drybag – keeps your technical equipment dry
- [ ] ZipLoc bags help you organize your food

2) Clothes

Compared to city trips, you need to pack more functional clothes because of the weather conditions, which can change quickly in this region.

Moreover, you should invest in some good outdoor clothes that are comfortable but also easy to handle. I plan for only a few days. After or in between I wash my clothes. This ensures I pack lightweight.

- [ ] 4x underwear
- [ ] 2x socks
- [ ] 3x t-shirts (mid layer) – I recommend using breathable sports shirts
- [ ] 1x hiking pants, with the option to turn into a short pant
- [ ] 1x rain pants (optional)
- [ ] 1x fleece jacket (mid layer) – highly recommended for colder parts and the evenings!
- [ ] 1x breathable, waterproof jacket as a shell layer
- [ ] 1x scarf – for cold and windy parts
- [ ] 1x hat/beanie

Consider: I focused on the summer season. For winter, you should add at least one layer and exchange shirts for warmer clothes!

If you don't mind getting wet, you can also go without rainproof gear and take some spare dry clothes for the campsite (which you never use anywhere else than in dry surroundings!)

3) Toiletries

As you are out in nature most of the time, keep it simple. When you're back to civilization, you'll have all amenities in your hotel or you can buy your favorite products in the next shop.

- [ ] 1x toothbrush and toothpaste
- [ ] 1-2x soap (lightweight, easy to handle), simply the best when you're in nature
- [ ] 1x basic skin cream
- [ ] 1x sunscreen
- [ ] 1x roll of toilet paper
- [ ] 1x microfiber towel - dries super fast, lightweight and small

4) Trekking Gear

- [ ] 1x sunglasses
- [ ] 1x good hiking boots, preferably waterproof
- [ ] foldable drinking bottle, saves space and weight
- [ ] optional: hiking poles, not needed but they can be very helpful

5) Camping Gear & Cooking

Camping in Patagonia means being prepared for rough weather conditions.

Your tent should be durable. Because of the strong winds, I recommend using one with aluminum poles as other materials tend to break more easily!

- [ ] 1x tent – the tents from MSR are high quality and come with aluminum poles.
- [ ] 1x mat – to protect from hard and cold underground
- [ ] 1x sleeping bag – preferably small, lightweight but still warm
- [ ] 1x pair of flip-flops – to use in the camp after a long day in your hiking boots
- [ ] 1x head lamp – you will need it in the night!
- [ ] 1x stove – preferably for gas cans
- [ ] 2x gas cans – you can mostly buy them in the town/village at the spot (Puerto Natales, Calafate, El Chalten, Bariloche, Punta Arenas)
- [ ] 1x pot – you'll use it for everything: preparing meals and cooking water
- [ ] 1x plate, fork, spoon, knife
- [ ] 1x metal cup
- [ ] 2x lighter & matches (as a fallback option)

Backpacking in Chile

6) Food

My main focus was to pack as lightly as possible because food will be the heaviest part of the Patagonia Packing List. Consider taking the following in your backpack:

- [ ] Breakfast: porridge and dry fruits, tea bags/instant coffee
- [ ] Lunch: cereal bars, nuts, dry fruits and Snickers
- [ ] Dinner: rice / pasta plus sauce powder, salami and cheese to add flavor
- [ ] Chocolate & Candies
- [ ] A small plastic bottle of alcohol (evening and for celebrations) ;)
- [ ] Another option is to take lightweight prepared meals!

7) Tools & Gadgets

- [ ] Multi Tool – to fix stuff or for preparing your meals (all-in-one!)
- [ ] External battery – to charge camera/devices
- [ ] GoPro – great waterproof camera for the outdoors (bring extra batteries!)
- [ ] GorillaPod – small, lightweight tripod to use with your camera
- [ ] Solar-charger

Notes:

Trekking Guide "W" Route

The W in Torres del Paine is the most popular multi-day hike as you come to see most of the highlights of the park. If you have a look at the map of the trail, you'll quickly realize why it is called the W trek (red part of the trail).

I'll first explain the standard route and then give examples of longer & shorter itineraries. Always plan your trips regarding your physical ability and your experience.

If you have little or no hiking experience, keep it low and plan more time for each trek!

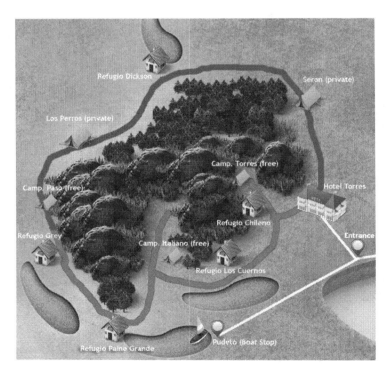

The ‚W' is the part from Refugio Grey to Hotel Las Torres

1) The W in 5 days, 4 nights (100 km, around 72,300 CLP)

This is the perfect schedule for a relaxed time in the park starting with a nice boat trip and the Glacier Grey and finishing with the sunrise at the Torres in the morning of the last day.

The start and finish are always Puerto Natales. All prices are in Chilean pesos.

Day 1: Puerto Natales - Refugio Grey
(11 km, 18.000 CLP + 15.000 CLP + 15.000 CLP + 6.000 CLP)

Leave Puerto Natales with the early bus (15.000 CLP return ticket) and get off at Pudeto (next stop after the park entrance – fee: 18.000 CLP) where you catch the catamaran to Paine Grande (15.000 CLP).

Use the waiting time to visit the waterfall nearby (ask for the time of the boat before leaving).

After your arrival in Paine Grande start walking to Refugio Grey. The path goes uphill along the Lago Grey with some lookouts on the way. The whole trek will take around 3-4 hours so you'll arrive in the afternoon. Then, you can set up your tent (6.000 CLP) and have dinner.

If you have some time left, you can go down to the beach and maybe touch some icebergs.

Backpacking in Chile

Day 2: Glacier Grey – Paine Grande (19 km, 7,000 CLP)

Get up early, leave your stuff at the camp, and just take a day pack to hike up to Paso (at 8:00 a.m.). After around 1-1.5 hours you'll reach a former campsite (signs with "no camping") with a lookout nearby (you can see a small path that leads to the platform, hard to find!)—time to enjoy the view to the glacier for a while (9:30 a.m. – 10:00 a.m.).

Now, you can decide if you want to continue a bit more in the direction of Paso or keep it shorter. The good thing about the way to Paso is that you'll have great views to the glacier and see a bit more of the massive southern icefield. The downside is that it's uphill and adds more km to your trek (on top of the mentioned 19 km). Do not go all the way up to Paso as it is a pretty long walk (you have to get back to Paine Grande today on time to be fit for the next day).

After your return to Refugio Grey at around lunchtime (12 / 1 p.m.) pack your stuff and head back down (at around 1 / 2 p.m.) to Paine Grande where you spent the night (7.000 CLP). It will take around 3-4 hours. Ensure that you find a nice place next to the little hill to avoid a bit of the massive winds down there.

Day 3: Valle del Frances – Los Cuernos (28 km, 8,500 CLP)

Today is a long and tough day, so get up early again and walk (start at 8:00 a.m.) to Campamento Italiano (around two hours = 10 a.m.). Leave your big backpack at the camp and head to the Mirador Frances with your daypack (take lunch, water, sun cream).

After 2.5 hours you'll reach the Mirador and have lunch (12:30 p.m.). Go back down to Italiano, grab your backpack, and keep going to Los Cuernos (03:00 / 3:30 p.m.). Another two hours later, you should reach the campsite (at 5:00/5:30 p.m. – 8.500 CLP).

Day 4: Los Cuernos – Campamento Torres (20 km, free)

On your last full day, you have a nice hike ahead – starting flat and going up at the end to the base of the Torres. Start your walk around 9 a.m. to Campamento Chileno.

The trail goes along the Lago Nordernskjöld. After around 3.5 hours, you'll reach the shortcut to Chileno (it's hard to miss as there is a big sign saying "shortcut to Chileno").

Another two hours later, you'll arrive at the Refugio Chileno (around 2:30 p.m./3 p.m.) you can make a short break and head uphill to the free campsite Campamento Torres afterward. This will take around one hour.

After setting up your tent, use the chance to visit the Torres for the first time — it's a 45 min walk uphill.

Go to bed early today, as you have to get up early tomorrow to see the sunrise at the towers. Depending on the time of the sunrise (ask the rangers) set your alarm 1–1.5 hours before and prepare a daypack with a mat, sleeping bag, and breakfast, as well as rain jacket).

Day 5: Torres – Puerto Natales
(16 – 23,5 km, 2.800 CLP optional)

In summer, the sunrise is around 6 a.m. Therefore, leave the camp with your daypack at 5 a.m. to arrive at the Mirador of the Towers on time. Set up your little picnic and enjoy. If you are lucky, you'll see amazing colors with a clear view and have the best breakfast ever. If you are not lucky, you'll have rain and clouds. In that case, you'll love that you've been up here the day before.

Don't make the mistake to skip the way up when it is raining in the camp: the weather changes really quickly and you might regret it later. Go for it anyway, as it is your last day and it doesn't matter if your sleeping bag gets wet up there!

After your return, take down your tent, pack your stuff, and leave the camp at around 9 a.m. Head down to the Hotel Las Torres. It'll take around three hours to arrive there.

Depending on the time you arrive (should be 12 p.m.), you can decide if you want to walk from the Hotel to the entrance (one hour, 7,5 km along the road) or pay 2,500 CLP extra to take the minibus, which leaves around 2 p.m. The bus back to Puerto Natales leaves at 2:30 p.m. from the entrance, as already described in the preparation guide.

Congratulations!
You've done the W in Torres del Paine and with that around 100 km by foot.

2) The W in 4 days, 3 nights (100 km, around 66,300 CLP)

If you are short on time but good in shape, you can also do the whole 'W' in one day less.

For this, you simply complete Day 1 and Day 2 in one day. With this, you have a real challenging program right at the start.

Day 1: Puerto Natales – Refugio Grey – Paine Grande (28 - 30 km, 18.000 CLP + 15.000 CLP + 15.000 CLP + 7.000 CLP)

Leave Puerto Natales with the early bus (15.000 CLP return ticket) and get off at Pudeto (the next stop after the park entrance – fee: 18.000 CLP) where you catch the catamaran to Paine Grande (15.000 CLP). Use the waiting time to visit the waterfall nearby (ask for the time of the boat before leaving).

After your arrival in Paine Grande, leave your things at the camp and take a day pack to hike up to the Refugio Grey. The path goes uphill along the Lago Grey with some lookouts on the way. The whole trek will take around 3-4 hours, so you'll arrive in the afternoon (4 p.m.). Keep walking in the direction of Paso.

After around 1-1.5 hours, you'll reach a former campsite with a lookout nearby—time to enjoy the view of the glacier (5 p.m.). Do not continue the way up to Paso as it is a pretty long walk (you have to get back to Paine Grande today to be fit for the next day).

After your return to Refugio Grey (6 p.m.) head back down to Paine Grande where you spent the night (7.000 CLP). It will take around three hours. Ensure you find a nice place next to the little hill for your tent to avoid a bit of the massive winds down there.

>> Continue with Day 3 of the previous itinerary

3) The W in 6 days, 5 nights (100 km, around 72.300 CLP)

So, you decided to take it easy and enjoy a day more in this amazing park? Great, I guess you'll not regret it and you have a bit more time for lookouts and pictures.

For stretching your stay, it's best to split the very tough 3rd day and change the stops afterward a bit. Therefore, start with the standard itinerary and continue on Day 3 with this:

Day 3: Valle del Frances – Campamento Italiano (22,5 km, free)

You don't need to get up early today (start at 10:00 a.m.) for Campamento Italiano (around two hours = 12 p.m.). leave your big backpack at the camp and head to the Mirador Frances with your daypack (take lunch, water, sun cream).

After 2.5 hours, you'll reach the Mirador and have a late lunch (2:30 p.m.).

Return to Italiano and get your tent ready for the night. As it is a free campsite, you don't have to pay tonight.

Day 4: Campamento Italiano – Refugio Chileno (19 km, 8,500 CLP)

Again, you can take it easy. Start your walk around 10 a.m. to Refugio Chileno.

The trail goes along the Lago Nordernskjöld. After around 5.5 hours, you'll reach the shortcut to Chileno (it's hard to miss, as there is a big sign saying "shortcut to Chileno").

Another two hours later, you'll arrive at the Refugio Chileno (around 5:30 p.m.).

Day 5: Refugio Chileno – Campamento Torres (8 km, free)

As you see, you have the most relaxed day ahead because you just move from one campsite to another. Have a slow start and head uphill, set up your tent and use the huge amount of time to spend some hours at the Torres in the afternoon.

Go to bed early today as you have to get up very early tomorrow to see the sunrise at the towers. Depending on the time of the sunrise (ask the rangers) set your alarm 1 – 1.5 hours before and prepare a daypack with a mat, sleeping bag, and breakfast as well as a rain jacket)

Consider: Torres is very popular. Therefore, you can stay mostly only for one night there.

>> **For Day 6, continue with Day 5 of the standard itinerary.**

Trekking Guide "O" / Circuit Route

If you are in Patagonia, you should spend as much time as possible out there in nature. Therefore, the Circuit Trail in Torres del Paine is the perfect trekking option for experiencing the full awesomeness of the park, including the southern ice field as the absolute highlight.

As in the other guides for the shorter W trail, I'll first explain the standard route and then give examples of longer and shorter itineraries afterward. Please plan your trips always with regard to your physical ability and your experience. If you have little or no hiking experience, keep it low and plan more time for each trek.

The path shown represents the full circuit a.k.a. the ‚O'

Please Note:

Since 2016, the CONAF limits the number of people on the circuit to 80 per day and you are only allowed to hike it counterclockwise. Make sure to reserve all the campsites in advance and have some sort of booking confirmation with you to prove it (they only allow people with reservations to do the hike as the camp spots are limited).

1) The circuit (a.k.a. 'O') in 8 days, 7 nights (130 km, around 71.800 CLP)

With the standard itinerary, you will have the big experience of hiking Torres del Paine without being in a rush. The first days are pretty relaxed and perfect for getting used to the whole hiking thing.

Nevertheless, I recommend planning always one day more—sometimes the John Gardner Pass is not doable because of very bad weather conditions. In that case, you might have to go back and stay one night more at Campamento Los Perros (make sure to take some extra food with you).

Moreover, I describe everything with stays in campsites/campsites next to refugios (it's not possible to do the described trek with refugio stays only).

Day 1: Puerto Natales – Campamento Serón (12 km, 15.000 CLP + 18.000 CLP + 8.500 CLP)

Leave Puerto Natales with the early bus (15.000 CLP return ticket), get off at the park entrance (fee: 18.000 CLP), and start walking. Head to the river and cross it. Walk along the street until you see a path to your right that goes to Serón.

After a nice walk through the woods and open grasslands, you arrive at Campamento Serón in the early afternoon. We keep it low for today and start setting up the tent for the night (8.500 CLP).

Day 2: Campamento Serón – Refugio Dickson (18 km, 6.000 CLP)

Today, you'll have to walk only a bit more than yesterday to get to the most beautiful campsite in the park. Because you'll walk for approximately five hours you can get up late, pack your stuff, and leave the camp after having a relaxed breakfast.

The path goes along a river and little lakes and heads uphill over a little pass where you can experience heavy winds.

Depending on the time you left, Serón you'll arrive in the afternoon at Lake Dickson where you find a campsite located directly on the river with a glacier in the background.

Day 3: Refugio Dickson – Campamento Los Perros (11 km, 6.000 CLP)

Isn't it beautiful here? As you see, you have another short, nice walk ahead and enough time to enjoy the scenery at Dickson for a bit longer and a nice breakfast at the mirador before you get ready to hike.

Start your hike to Los Perros at around 11 a.m. You'll hike a bit uphill and through the forest before you reach a mirador with a nice view back to the Lago Dickson area and to the valley you are supposed to walk up. A bit later, you have the chance of seeing a waterfall (you'll hear when you are next to it).

Keep going after a short break. The path leads through a forest and after that you'll cross the river twice. Now it goes up, across stones, and rocks—believe me, it's worth it!

Up there, you reach the Mirador Britanico with a great view to the Glacier Los Perros and the glacier lake. Take your time as the campsite is only a 10-15min walk from here.

With all the breaks, you'll reach Los Perros between 3 p.m. and 4 p.m. Go to bed early today; the steepest part awaits you tomorrow. Set your alarm for 5 a.m. (summer season), as it is best to cross the pass in the morning.

Day 4: Campamento Los Perros – Paso (12 km, free)

Oh, 5 a.m. it's still dark and cold, which makes you want to stay in your warm sleeping bag. Try to resist and head out to treat yourself with a nice breakfast and a hot coffee to be ready for the tough pass. After packing again—now you should be an expert in doing that—leave the camp (6 a.m.) and head uphill for the next 2-3 hours.

After walking through the woods, you'll reach an open area where you basically walk on stones and rocks. Before continuing, make sure the weather conditions are good enough to see the orange/red poles that mark the trail. If not, turn around and head back as it might be too dangerous to continue (it gets much rougher the higher you get).

If everything is fine, you will have an amazing walk, though it might be exhausting walking uphill and experiencing the strong winds. When you reach the highest point, chances are high that you will have to crouch because of strong winds. You can find wind cover on the left-hand side to celebrate the climb.

When continuing, the wind will calm down but your breath will be taken away by the stunning view you'll have for the next hour. Enjoy it and 5-6 hours after you left Los Perros you should arrive at Campamento Paso (11 a.m. – 12 a.m.) where you can enjoy some views nearby and have enough time to charge your batteries.

Backpacking in Chile

Day 5: Campamento Paso – Refugio Grey – Paine Grande (21 km, 7.000 CLP)

Wow – day number five and you already experienced a lot of cool stuff, eh? Stay excited and leave the camp around 8 a.m.

It took me five hours to walk to Refugio Grey and it was my personal highlight as you walk along the cliffs right next to Glacier Grey. Moreover, you have to climb some ladders and cross some bridges. Three to four hours after you leave Paso, you arrive at an old campsite. Here, you should use the chance to visit the Mirador nearby and continue afterward to Refugio Grey where you can have lunch (arrival around 1 p.m.).

Pack your stuff and head back down (at around 2 p.m.) to Paine Grande where you spent the night (7,000 CLP). It will take around 3-4 hours. Ensure you find a nice place next to the little hill to avoid the massive winds down there.

Day 6: Valle del Frances – Los Cuernos (22,5 km, 8.500 CLP)

Today is a long and tough day, so get up early again and walk (start at 8:00 a.m.) to Campamento Italiano (around 2 hours = 10 a.m.).

Leave your big backpack at the camp and head to the Mirador Frances with your daypack (take lunch, water, and sun cream).

After 2.5 hours, you'll reach the mirador and have lunch (12:30 p.m.). Go back down to Italiano, grab your backpack, and keep going to Los Cuernos (3:00/3:30 p.m.).

After another two hours, you should reach the campsite (at 5:00/5:30 p.m. – 8,500 CLP).

Day 7: Los Cuernos – Campamento Torres
(20 km, free but reservation mandatory)

On your last full day, you have a nice hike ahead—starting flat and going up at the end to the base of the Torres. Start your walk around 9 a.m. to Campamento Chileno.

The trail goes along the Lago Nordernskjöld, after around 3.5 hours you'll reach the shortcut to Chileno (it's hard to miss as there is a big sign saying "shortcut to Chileno").

Another two hours later, you'll arrive at the Refugio Chileno (around 2:30 p.m. / 3 p.m.). You can take a short break before heading uphill to the free campsite Campamento Torres. This will take around one hour. After setting up your tent, use the chance to visit the Torres for the first time—it's a 45 min walk uphill.

Go to bed early today, as you have to get up early tomorrow to see the sunrise at the towers. Depending on the time of the sunrise (ask the rangers) set your alarm 1 – 1.5 hours before and prepare a daypack with a mat, sleeping bag, breakfast, and a rain jacket)

Day 8: Torres – Puerto Natales (10 – 15 km, 2.800 CLP optional)

In summer, the sunrise is around 6 a.m. Therefore, leave the camp with your daypack at 5 a.m. to arrive at the Mirador of the Towers on time. Set up your little picnic and enjoy. If you are lucky, you'll see amazing colors on the towers (pink, orange, yellow) with a clear view, having the best breakfast ever. If you are not lucky you'll have rain and clouds. In that case, you'll love the fact that you've been up here the day before. Don't make the mistake to skip the way up when it is raining at the camp. The weather changes quickly and you might regret it later. Go for it anyway as it is your last day and it doesn't matter if your sleeping bag gets wet up there ;)

On your return, take down your tent, pack your things, and leave the camp at around 9 a.m. Head down to the Hotel Las Torres. It will take around three hours to arrive there. Depending on the time you arrive (should be 12 p.m.), you can decide if you want to walk from the hotel to the entrance (one hour, 7.5 km along the road) or pay 2,800 CLP extra to take the minibus, which leaves around 2 p.m.

The bus back to Puerto Natales leaves at 2:30 p.m. from the entrance, as already described in the preparation guide.

Congratulations!
You've done the circuit/'O' and with that around 125-130 km by foot.

2) The circuit in 7 days, 6 nights
(130 km, around 71.800 CLP)

Ok, you feel good. Have you done some hikes before or just have limited time? Then, you can also do the circuit in a day less.

Please consider taking food for an additional day as the pass might not be doable because of bad weather conditions.

Day 1: Pto. Natales – Campamento Serón
(12 km, 15.000 CLP + 18.000 CLP + 8.500 CLP)

See the standard itinerary.

Day 2: Campamento Serón – Refugio Dickson – Los Perros
(29 km, 6.000 CLP)

Today and tomorrow are quite challenging, so get a good breakfast and start early (7 a.m.) to get to the most beautiful campsite in the park around lunchtime.

The path goes along a river and little lakes before heading uphill over a little pass where you can experience heavy winds. You'll arrive at lunchtime at the Lago Dickson where you find a campsite located directly on the river with a glacier in the background (12 a.m.).

Isn't it beautiful here? As you see, you have another 9 km walk ahead. Enjoy the scenery at Dickson for a bit and have a nice lunch at the mirador before you get ready to hike (1 p.m.).

You'll hike a bit uphill and through the forest before you reach a mirador with a nice view back to the Lago Dickson area and to the valley you are supposed to walk up. A bit later, you have the chance of seeing a waterfall (you'll hear when you are next to it).

The path leads through a forest and, after that, you'll cross the river twice. Now it goes up, across stones and rocks—believe me, it's worth it!

Up there, you reach the Mirador Britanico with a great view to the glacier Los Perros and the glacier lake. Take your time as the campsite is only a 10-15min walk from here.

With all the breaks, you'll reach Los Perros between 6 – 7 p.m.. Go to bed early today, as the steepest part awaits you tomorrow. Set your alarm to 5 a.m., as it is best to cross the pass in the morning.

Day 3: Campamento Los Perros – Paso – Refugio Grey (22 km, 6.000 CLP)

Oh, 5 a.m.—it's still dark and cold, which makes you want to stay in your warm sleeping bag. Try to resist and head out to treat yourself to a nice breakfast and a hot coffee to be ready for the tough pass. After packing again—now you should be an expert in doing that—you leave the camp (6 a.m.) and head uphill for the next 2-3 hours.

After walking through the woods, you'll reach an open area where you basically walk on stones and rocks. Before continuing, make sure the weather conditions are good enough to see the orange/red poles that mark the trail. If not, turn around and head back as it might be too dangerous to continue (it gets much rougher the higher you get).

If everything is fine, you will have an amazing walk, though it might be exhausting walking uphill and experiencing the strong winds. When you reach the highest point, chances are high that you have to crouch because of strong winds. You can find wind cover on the left-hand side to celebrate the climb. The wind will calm down but your breath will be taken away by the stunning view you'll have for the next hour. Enjoy it. Five to six hours after you left Los Perros you should arrive at Campamento Paso (11 a.m. – 12 a.m.) to charge your batteries before you continue to Grey.

It took me five hours to walk to Refugio Grey and it was my personal highlight as you walk along the cliffs right next to Glacier Grey. Moreover, you have to climb some ladders and cross some bridges. Three to four hours after you leave Paso, you will arrive at an old campsite. Use the chance to visit the mirador nearby and continue afterward to the Refugio Grey where you'll spend the night (arrival around 5 p.m., 6,000 CLP).

Day 4: Refugio Grey – Paine Grande (11 km, 7,000 CLP)

Yes, the last two days have been exhausting. Use this day to relax a bit so you have enough power for the upcoming highlights. Therefore, you can sleep longer and have a long breakfast.

Pack your stuff and head down (at around 11 a.m.) to Paine Grande where you spend the night (7,000 CLP), it will take around 3-4 hours. Ensure you find a nice place next to the little hill to avoid a bit of the massive winds down there.

>> Continue with Day 6 of the standard itinerary

3) The circuit in 9 days, 8 nights
(130 km, around 71,800 CLP)

Ok, you can't get enough and want to have a really relaxed trekking adventure—use this itinerary to enjoy it the best way.

For stretching your stay, it's best to split day number 6 and change the stops afterward a bit.

Therefore start with the standard itinerary and continue on Day 6 with this:

Day 6: Valle del Frances – Campamento Italiano
(17.5 km, free but reservation needed)

You don't need to get up so early today (start at 10:00 a.m.) for Campamento Italiano (around 2 hours = 12 p.m.). Leave your big backpack at the camp and head to the Mirador Frances with your daypack (take lunch, water, and sun cream).

After 2.5 hours, you'll reach the Mirador and have a late lunch (14:30 p.m.). Go back down to Italiano and get your tent ready for the night. As it is a free campsite, you don't have to pay tonight.

Day 7: Campamento Italiano – Refugio Chileno
(22 km, 8.500 CLP but reservation needed)

Again, you can take it easy. Start your walk around 10 a.m. to Campamento Chileno. The trail goes along the Lago Nordernskjöld. After around 5.5 hours, you'll reach the shortcut to Chileno (it's hard to miss as there is a big sign saying "shortcut to Chileno"). Another two hours later, you'll arrive at the Refugio Chileno (around 5:30 p.m.).

**Day 8: Refugio Chileno – Campamento Torres
(5 km, free but reservation needed)**

You have the most relaxed day ahead because you will just move from one campsite to another. Have a slow start and head uphill, set up your tent, and use the huge amount of time to spend some hours at the Torres in the afternoon.

Go to bed early today as you have to get up early tomorrow to see the sunrise at the towers. Depending on the time of the sunrise (ask the rangers) set your alarm 1 – 1.5 hours before and prepare a daypack with a mat, sleeping bag, and breakfast, as well as a rain jacket.

Consider: Torres is very popular. Therefore, you can stay mostly for only one night there.

For Day 9, continue with Day 8 of the standard itinerary.

6 ADDITIONAL RESOURCES

All URLs mentioned in this book

As it is not possible to link directly from a book to a website, I offer the option to request the eBook for free (see Preface) and I created the following website/link list with all important resources:

www.back-packer.org/chile-book-links/

Recommended Guidebooks

If you want to come well prepared, the following guides are great resources for Chile, which I also used during my time:

Chile & Easter Island, Lonely Planet

The Lonely Planet for Chile covers also Patagonia and lines out the most popular things to do. It comes with small maps of the covered cities/villages and gives recommendations on restaurants and places to stay.

Trekking Patagonia, Lonely Planet

This is a must if you plan to hike a few times in Patagonia as this guide has itineraries for several parts of Patagonia and even for Tierra del Fuego. It's a good resource for the popular spots like Torres del Paine and Chaltén, as well as the lesser-known parts. Highly recommended!

The Carretera Austral: A Guide to One of the World's Most Scenic Road Trips

This is the first guidebook focused entirely on the magnificent and historic road uniting northern and southern Patagonia. In addition to practical advice, the book explores the mythical history of the region and the social and economic impact of the relatively recent connectivity to both Chile and Argentina.

DK Eyewitness Travel Guide: Chile & Easter Island

The fully updated guide includes unique cutaways, floor plans, and reconstruction of the must-see sites, plus street-by-street maps of fascinating cities and towns. The new-look guide is also packed with photographs and illustrations leading you straight to the best attractions on offer.

Lonely Planet South America on a shoestring

This Lonely Planet is also available as a Kindle eBook and covers highlights in Argentina, Bolivia, Brazil, Chile, Colombia, and Peru. It offers essential information at your fingertips, including hours of operation, phone numbers, websites, transit tips, and prices.

Lonely Planet Latin American Spanish Phrasebook & Dictionary

Get More From Your Trip with Easy-to-Find Phrases for Every Travel Situation – the Lonely Planet Phrasebook helps you to order the right meal with the menu decoder and comes with a 3500-word two-way dictionary. Moreover, you'll find shortcuts, key phrases, and common Q&As.

Recommended Maps

I used the following maps to navigate during my time in Patagonia.

Torres del Paine Trekking Map (waterproof)

I used this map to prepare my itinerary in Torres del Paine, Chile. As it is a waterproof map, it is also great to use it on the trek!

El Chaltén Trekking Map (Fitz Roy, Cerro Torre)

If you plan to hike around the Argentinean trekking capital El Chaltén, this is the right map to buy. It even covers the border crossing to get to the starting point of the Chilean Carretera Austral in the north!

Other Guide Books from Me

If you plan on traveling to the neighboring Argentina, you should consider getting my travel guide for this country as well —it is similarly structured:

Backpacking in Argentina: My Argentina Travel Guide

The book includes travel guides for the several regions of Argentina as well as a tiny trekking guide for El Chaltén and Ushuaia. Checklists are included to help make sure you don't forget anything.

This eBook is designed to save you a lot of time and make your trip much easier. Download it now and take it with you!

7 ABOUT THE AUTHOR

My name is Steve, I'm an information architect turned travel filmmaker and blogger from Hamburg in Germany. In my South America travel guides, I share personal tips, recommendations, and experiences I explored on my travels.

Beside my work as an author, I have my own international TV show format at DW TV as part of the travel show "Check-In". Additionally, I publish new travel videos regularly on my own YouTube channel called "Backpacker Steve".

About Back-Packer.org

I created this travel blog to provide practical information and tips you need to prepare for your next trip. From things to do, the gear you need, and places to eat at to recommended accommodations.

Furthermore, I share my own travel experiences, such as travel advice, how to save money for traveling, how to connect work and travel, and which destinations are worth a visit. Make sure to check out my blog for further travel inspiration!

Copyright © 2017 by Steve Hänisch,
Website: www.back-packer.org

All rights reserved.

No part of this book may be reproduced in any form or by any electronic or mechanical means including information storage and retrieval systems without permission in writing from the author. The only exception is by a reviewer, who may quote short excerpts in a review.

All Photos by Steve Hänisch

Although the author and publisher have made every effort to ensure that the information in this book was correct at press time, the author and publisher do not assume and hereby disclaim any liability to any party for any loss, damage, or disruption caused by errors or omissions, whether such errors or omissions result from negligence, accident, or any other cause.

The information provided within this book is for general informational purposes only. While we try to keep the information up-to-date and correct, there are no representations or warranties, express or implied, about the completeness, accuracy, reliability, suitability or availability with respect to the information, products, services, or related graphics contained in this book for any purpose. Any use of this information is at your own risk.

The authors and publisher advise readers to take full responsibility for their safety and know their limits. Before practicing the outdoor activities described in this book, be sure that your equipment is well maintained, and do not take risks beyond your level of experience, aptitude, training, and comfort level.

ISBN: 1545126313
ISBN-13: 978-1545126318

Made in Germany
Second edition, April 2017

Made in the USA
Middletown, DE
01 July 2017